PATHWAYS *OF* PRAYER

Torn Curtain Publishing
Wellington, New Zealand
www.torncurtainpublishing.com

ISBN Softcover 978-0-473-67978-1
ISBN EPub 978-0-473-67979-8

Unless otherwise indicated, all Scripture quotations are taken from the Holy Bible, New King James Version. Copyright © 1982 by Thomas Nelson, Inc. Used by permission. All rights reserved.

Scripture quotations marked (NIV) are taken from the Holy Bible, New International Version®, NIV®. Copyright © 1973, 1978, 1984, 2011 by Biblica, Inc.™ Used by permission of Zondervan. All rights reserved worldwide. www.zondervan.com

Scripture quotations marked MSG are taken from THE MESSAGE, copyright © 1993, 2002, 2018 by Eugene H. Peterson. Used by permission of NavPress. All rights reserved. Represented by Tyndale House Publishers, a Division of Tyndale House Ministries.

Illustrations and cover design by Mikayla Monk. Used with permission.

Cataloguing in Publishing Data
Title: Pathways of Prayer
Author: Helen Monk
Subjects: Christian Living, Devotional, Prayer.

A copy of this title is held at the National Library of New Zealand.

PA*TH*WAYS *OF* *PR*AYER

HELEN MONK

AUTHOR'S NOTE

Prayer is my life, my 'heartbeat', my joy, and my vital connection to my heavenly Father through my Saviour, Jesus Christ. This book is produced from the overflow of my heart to encourage you in the exercise of prayer—our rite of passage as a child of God.

Pathways of Prayer emphasizes that there are many ways to pray, not just one standard liturgical method as you may have imagined, but a freedom of personal expression—ways to approach, acknowledge and connect with our loving God and to honour Him for who He is. Prayer is not a duty, nor a heavy responsibility, but a 'way of being' as a child of God. It's the most natural outflow from the most important relationship in our life. Prayer is a mood, a mode, a way of being, a heart conviction and connection with the greatest source of life ever, our Creator, God.

Maybe you have struggled in your Christian journey to establish a good and consistent prayer life. As you read the pages in this book, my hope is that your heart will be stirred with sincere desire to connect in a more meaningful and natural way with God Himself. Through prayer you will discover His heartbeat for you and His strength and power enabling you to live your best life here on earth. Matthew 11:30 puts it this way: "Keep company with me and you'll learn how to live feely and lightly"(MSG).

There is inspiration, revelation, power, healing and enlargement of faith on the other side of our prayer and petitions as we invite Jesus into every space in our life. What a privilege we have been granted to personally access God's throne of grace!

Many blessings to you, dear readers. You are in my prayers!

Love, Helen x

This book is made up of fifty-two entries in reference to the fifty-two days it took Nehemiah to rebuild the wall around Jerusalem. May I suggest, however, rather than reading the devotions in fifty-two days, take your time and read one per week, reflecting and meditating on the prayer you recorded over the full seven days.

CONTENTS

PART 1: PRAYER HELPS

PART 2: PRAYER CONNECTS

PART 3: PRAYER EMBRACES

PART 4: PRAYER TRIUMPHS

PART 5: PRAYER PROMPTS

PART ONE
PRAYER HELPS

I will lift up my eyes to the hills—From whence comes my help?
My help comes from the Lord, who made heaven and earth.
Psalm 121v1&2

1

HELP, LORD!

*Seek the Lord while He may be found, call
upon Him while He is near.*
Isaiah 55v6

MY PERSONAL JOURNEY OF prayer began at approximately five years of age. At the time, I had no understanding of Christianity, yet I instinctively knew I needed to cry out to God—to ask for His help, not because I was in danger, but purely because of an innate awareness of, and sensitivity to, His presence. I had no doubt that a great God existed who was totally there for me. I simply called out to Him in childlike faith. Over the years that followed, my faith and understanding developed as I made significant commitments to fully follow Him.

Regardless of whether we reach out to God at a young age or later in life, God always responds to our cries for help. Our prayers, however simple, are a statement of faith and trust in His ability to save us, strengthen us, and outwork His will through our lives.

In the book of James we read of Christians who resorted to fighting and coveting in their desire to obtain what they wanted. They could have accessed God's help to overcome the lust in their hearts, but instead they chose to tackle their felt needs on a carnal level. They allowed a self-centred cry to drown out a God-focused prayer of faith. In his letter, James chides the warring Christians with these words:

You do not have because you do not ask.
James 4v2

We *miss out* when we fail to *cry out* to God! But when we simply present our needs to God, He surrounds us with His help, deliverance and provision.

I can testify strongly to God's help throughout the journey of my life. As a young child, God provided what my heart needed—closeness with Himself, and a place of learning through a home-based children's Bible Club that *just happened* to commence down the road from our farm in the remote countryside of rural New Zealand. How amazing was that? God is so strategic! And, our only neighbour *just happened* to invite my sisters and I to come regularly to a children's 'Happy Hour' outreach run by one of the local churches in a marquee at nearby Otaki Beach. My young heart sang for joy in the atmosphere of faith and worship, my spirit fully soaking in the revelation of Jesus.

Throughout my childhood, God always came through in response to my cries for help—even during school exams! Doing well was important to me. On one occasion, I became tangibly aware of His presence standing right behind my chair in the exam hall and opening pages of curriculum before my eyes. It was a phenomenal experience!

I have much to say regarding God's faithfulness to respond to my cries as a young person—even in bringing me together in marriage with someone who loved God. In the early days of our relationship we had still not fully grasped the extent of God's plan for our life together, but as a couple and as individuals, we asked for God's help on a daily basis, and we continue to do so, knowing that He alone strengthens us and enables us to be all He has called us to be.

> *If any of you lacks wisdom, let him ask of God, who gives to all*
> *liberally and without reproach, and it will be given to him. But*
> *let him ask in faith, with no doubting, for he who doubts is like*
> *a wave of the sea driven and tossed by the wind. For let not that*
> *man suppose that he will receive anything from the Lord; he is a*
> *double-minded man, unstable in all his ways.*
> *James 1v5-8*

What do you need to ask God for help with today? In response to your cry for help, God will come near to you, surround you, and provide for you. If you have a need, then that's the beginning of a great prayer life right there! "Help, Lord!" is such a legitimate prayer!

P AUSE AND REFLECT. Is there an area of your life where you need help?

R ECORD your requests for God's intervention.

A CKNOWLEDGE in prayer that God is listening and is so willing to help you in your need.

Y IELD YOUR CONCERNS completely to Him, thanking God that He will fully act on your behalf.

2

WHAT'S HAPPENING HERE?

*"No weapon formed against you shall prosper, and every tongue
which rises against you in judgment you shall condemn. This is
the heritage of the servants of the Lord, and their righteousness
is from Me," says the Lord.
Isaiah 54v17*

GROWING UP, I ENJOYED close communion with Jesus and had created an
ethos of 'nice' around my life, including everything that flowed from my
Christianity. After all, I had experienced God's kindness and gentleness
toward me, His constant help, and His great encouragement. There was
no room in my thinking for the darker side of spiritual realities, or the
strongholds that exist in our world. I had just one category in my 'spiritual
reference'. But with ministry life approaching, I needed to be awoken to the
fact that we live amongst opposing forces.

The first incident didn't rock my personal world too much, but served to
bring an awareness to my soul that an adversary exists and is greatly provoked
when we step out in faith. When we position ourselves in obedience, we will
often experience a 'push back' in the spirit from any force that has gained a
foothold in the past. I was about to discover that any trouble we may encounter,
particularly if it is bizarre in nature, may be due to the fact that a collision
of kingdoms is happening—a clash in the spiritual realm!

When my husband, Bruce, and I decided to leave our farming to become
more active in fulltime ministry, 'all hell broke loose' on the family farm—in
particular, our very healthy livestock began to prematurely abort their calves,
resulting in an alarming number of deaths. The vet was perplexed. Why was

this happening? There was no obvious reason for what was taking place.

When there is no answer in the natural, it is most likely spiritual.

Sure enough, *prayer revealed the answer!* God revealed to us that years previously an object known as a 'colour coil' had been stationed in one of the fields for the exact purpose of preventing cows from aborting their calves. How ironic!

Colour therapy is basically an occult practice. On our farm, previous generations had positioned colour coils, perceiving them to be a promise or guarantee of protection over the farm and livestock. However, any superstitious ritual not founded in the truth of Christ is a curse, and this curse, which had been given 'legal right' spiritually, rose up destructively just as we decided to step out in faith and serve God.

What did we do? We followed a simple process:

Remove the object. We simply extracted the coil from the ground and disposed of it.

Repent. We repented and sought forgiveness on behalf of those who had exposed the land to a curse, even in ignorance. Evil often parades itself as good, falsely promising health, protection and freedom, but ultimately it rises as a destructive curse, especially in the face of the advancement of the Gospel.

Renounce the spirit of deception. We renounced the lie that was associated with this practice, took authority in the name of Jesus, and gave the spirit of deception no permission to exist or operate on territory that belonged to the righteous.

Release. We released the land to function effectively and effortlessly under the anointing of the Spirit of God.

When we prayed and acted in this manner, the plague on our livestock, which had been present for many months, immediately stopped.

Whenever we realise an issue is far bigger than just the need for a heart or attitude change, we need to ask God, "What is happening here?" It's important to recognise that spiritual forces are at work, consistently and relentlessly opposing the work of God.

What needs to stop right now in your life? Has the enemy been given legal grounds to operate in your life and affairs due to fear and superstition? Has he gained a foothold on the 'land' of your health and wellbeing, your home and family, or your community? At what point was the enemy given access or granted the authority to dominate? Pray that God will reveal how the enemy has gained access. Resist him strongly in your faith, evict him using the process above, and take back the territory appointed for you to possess!

P AUSE AND CONSIDER. Is any illegal spiritual activity operating in your life?

R ECORD any unusual resistance you have experienced.

A CKNOWLEDGE the power of God to deliver you through prayer and repentance.

Y IELD your life and your possessions fully to the covering of Jesus.

3

UNWELCOME GUESTS

*Be sober, be vigilant; because your adversary the devil walks
about like a roaring lion, seeking whom he may devour. Resist
him, steadfast in the faith, knowing that the same sufferings are
experienced by your brotherhood in the world.*
1 Peter 5v8&9

ON ENTERING OUR FIRST appointment as pastors in a provincial city, our mindset was positive. We were believing that growth would come through our efforts, and we were ready for it. What we were not prepared for was the 'side swipe' we were quickly subjected to as we responded to this new mission. We had become aware of evil spirits through the unusual experience on the farm, but we were certainly not about to give the enemy any attention in our normal, everyday world!

We arrived in the city of Whanganui 'bright-eyed, bushy-tailed', and ready for the task ahead. Having just attended a leaders' conference in the country town of Waikanae, we felt equipped and readied for the position God had appointed us to. But another demonic encounter soon affirmed to us that the enemy was around and that he was threatened by our presence in the city.

In the early hours one night, Bruce woke and in an indistinct voice whimpered, ". . . I am going." A demonic force had taken hold of Bruce's throat and was threatening to take him out. The whole room was filled with fear and foreboding as we sensed he was slipping away. This was something we had never been exposed to—it was foreign territory for us, but Bruce had the presence of mind to say, "Helen, pray!" We began praying loudly in tongues, and as we did, the enemy released his grip from Bruce's neck and this frightening presence left our house.

"What just happened?" we asked. How could we, as a Christian family, be exposed to an invasion of this proportion from demonic spirits? Again, *prayer revealed the reason*!

We were living in rental accommodation at the time and soon discovered some 'occult' literature which had been left on a bookshelf belonging to the landlord. We knew that "a curse without a cause cannot land" (Proverbs 26v2), but here was a cause right under our nose that had gone undetected! Carefully we packed the books into the boxes, placed them in the unused garage, and prayerfully took authority over any lingering presence in the house. We certainly did not want to be subject to such spiritual force again, and by God's grace we weren't.

What the enemy used to frighten and intimidate us, God used to make us stronger. From that night on, we were able to more easily discern what we were up against and to minister in the powerful authority we experienced in Jesus' name.

Did it cause us to fear? *Not at all!* If anything, we were even more convinced of our mission and responsibility to free people and environments from *demonic residents and unwelcome visitors.* This experience transformed me personally from being somewhat dismissive of people's accounts of demonic activities, to someone God now used to discern and destroy demonic strongholds. Because I held no unhealthy fascination with the darker side of spiritual realities, God knew He could reveal them to me and trust me to deal with them as quickly as possible.

Many Christians are entertaining demonic forces without realising it. There are forces attached to ideals, philosophies, ethics, and morality that contravene the truth of God's Word. People are inviting demonic strongholds into their life through 'lifestyle choices', and God wants to open their eyes to this reality.

Have you encountered unwanted 'residents' and unwelcome 'guests' in your home or place of lodging? Have there been any disturbances that you have found hard to fathom? Is your heart at peace, or are you distressed by certain events and activities? Look around in prayer and discern if there are any unwelcome guests. If a counterfeit spirit is at work, use your authority to cast it out!

PAUSE AND REFLECT. Could there be any unwelcome visitors squatting on your land?

RECORD what spirit may be occupying space in the residence of your heart or mind.

ACKNOWLEDGE that you have been given all authority in the name of Jesus to evict the trespassers in prayer.

YIELD to God knowing He can restore peace and order in your environment.

4

BE FILLED

On the last day, that great day of the feast, Jesus stood and cried
out, saying, "If anyone thirsts, let him come to Me and drink.
He who believes in Me, as the scripture has said, out of his heart
will flow rivers of living water." But this He spoke concerning the
Spirit whom those believing in Him would receive; for the Holy
Spirit was not yet given, because Jesus was not yet glorified.
John 7v37-39

BEFORE HIS DEPARTURE FROM earth, Jesus encouraged His disciples to wait
for the 'Promise of the Father'—the Holy Spirit, our Helper (Acts 1:4, John
15:26). As God's children, we need the infilling of the Holy Spirit if we are
to be effective in the work God has called us to. In and of ourselves, we are
not capable of fulfilling supernatural assignments. Even in prayer, we don't
know how to pray unless the Holy Spirit leads us. We need Him to touch
our lives significantly and fill us with His power. God is so ready and willing
to pour out His Spirit when we thirst for more of Him!

To be filled with the Spirit of God involves a 'letting go' of control, pride,
embarrassment, resistance, or any basic fear. I invited Jesus into my life at a
very young age, and the moment I received Him as my Lord and Saviour, He
came and took up residence in my heart. This certainly happened through
the power of the Holy Spirit. But now the question was: Had the Holy Spirit
received *me*? Was I fully immersed in the Holy Spirit, as the scriptures
encourage (Matthew 3:11)?

I had always believed in God, but this was an aspect of the supernatural
I was yet to experience. My heart wasn't at all resistant—the problem was my

self-consciousness. I was shy, and fearful of embarrassing myself in front of others. But I was hungry for this experience, so I sought God privately for this amazing gift of being filled with the Holy Spirit. After all, how could I accomplish what He wanted for my life without fully knowing His power?

When our desire trumps our fears, results happen! As I prayed and sought God, He gently baptised me in His Holy Spirit—in my own home! I received what the Bible describes as 'peace that passes all understanding' (Philippians 4:7), and a quiet reassurance within.

For each of us, the manifestation of the baptism of the Holy Spirit will vary—the experience of some will be loud and joyful, while for others it may be peaceful and reassuring. As for the gift of tongues, in that moment at home I received a few words in the Spirit. While lamenting some months later that my heavenly language only consisted of four words, God prompted me very clearly to use the words I had, promising me that more would flow as I employed faith. You see, we need to *exercise what we have been given before we receive more!* This is true in many spheres of life. The more I began to use these four words consistently in prayer and praise, the more my spirit was freed, and soon a whole 'language' flowed out in response to my faith and 'letting go' of inhibitions.

I can testify that the gift of tongues has transformed me from being a self-conscious person to being completely uninhibited in the realm of prayer, where I strongly focus on the kingdom of God and release His power to heal and deliver. When I need encouragement, I speak in tongues; when I need discernment, I pray in tongues; when I desire breakthrough, I speak in tongues; when I feel fearful, I speak in tongues. When I simply want to worship, I speak (or sing) in tongues! This wonderful gift of the Holy Spirit edifies us and lifts us to greater realms in the Spirit where we are more conscious of what God desires than what we can comprehend with our own mind.

My prayer for you, dear reader, is that you may know the fullness of the Holy Spirit in your life enabling and empowering you to be the person God has called you to be.

P AUSE AND REFLECT. Have you received the fullness of the Holy Spirit?

R ECORD any area in which you need further release, and submit yourself to the Holy Spirit.

A CKNOWLEDGE God's generosity and His willingness to give His Holy Spirit to those who ask.

Y IELD your life fully to the infilling, guidance and leading of the Holy Spirit.

5

RECEIVE THE GIFT

*And it shall come to pass in the last days, says God, that I
will pour out of My Spirit on all flesh; Your sons and your
daughters shall prophesy, your young men shall see visions,
your old men shall dream dreams.*
Acts 2v17

I HAVE ENCOUNTERED PEOPLE who have sought prayer for the baptism of the
Holy Spirit many times, only to feel disappointed because they didn't receive
the gift of tongues, although they passionately desired it. Some continue to
respond to calls for prayer for the baptism of the Spirit, but disappointment
from what they have previously experienced subconsciously precedes them,
undermining any breakthrough they were hoping for. An almost foreboding
forecast is present, declaring: "I won't receive it," or "perhaps this gift is not
for me after all."

Though the experience is desired, negative expectation denies it. The truth
remains, however, that God has not withheld His Holy Spirit from anyone.
He has not limited His gifts to just a special few. This belief, held by some,
is a lie from the enemy to prevent people from experiencing God's fullness,
denying them the ability to operate at a new level supernaturally.

Here are some considerations to embrace as we come to receive the gift
of tongues:

Value the gift. The gift of tongues strengthens us, empowers us, reveals
mysteries to us, and is a form of direct communication with our heavenly
Father which the enemy cannot interpret or interrupt.

Realise tongues is a gift. A gift is a gift—we do not have to earn it!

13

God freely grants us the gift of the Holy Spirit to help us live an empowered Christian walk. We need to remove any distraction and focus just on Jesus. Closing our eyes while being prayed for is helpful in this manner. God is more desirous that you receive His gift than you are!

Employ faith. We just need to 'let go' and receive His gift for us by faith; however, faith also involves action. When we feel the Spirit of God overflowing in our lives, it is important that we release our spirit from within to praise Him with the sound of our heavenly language. The gift is present in seed form in every Christian, waiting to find an outward expression. But herein lies the problem for some: they are expecting 'a bolt from heaven' to make their lips move, forcing them to speak in another language! God could do that if He wanted, but instead He is looking for you and me to step out in faith and begin speaking, believing that the Holy Spirit will come behind us, releasing the words and sound. And so, I encourage you to simply begin by moving your mouth in faith! Some may hesitate when they hear themselves first speak in tongues because they cannot understand the language they are speaking. But the fact is, we are not supposed to understand—this is not an exercise of the mind, but an experience in the Spirit. We need to switch off our natural languages and speak from the depth of our spirit by faith!

To those who have experienced disappointment, I like to ask three questions to help find where the blockage may be:

1. *Has there been any occult involvement in your life that has not been repented of, which now is binding your will and spirit from fully receiving the gift of tongues?*

2. *Have you encountered teaching that opposes this spiritual experience? This is particularly prevalent where 'dispensation theology' has been taught, where speaking in tongues, miracles, healings and supernatural manifestations are deemed relevant only to the era when Jesus resided on earth, and are not for today.*

3. *Do you struggle with feelings of unworthiness? Some people fundamentally see themselves as unworthy, not good enough to*

receive the gift of the Holy Spirit. But the truth remains that God deems us all worthy to receive His Holy Spirit so we can prosper in life.

If you need breakthrough in the gift of tongues, consider if any of these three issues may be blocking your ability to believe and receive freely. Don't resort to logic or pessimism, but give your heart permission to respond openly and experience the supernatural infilling of the Holy Spirit. Today is a day of faith! Come on—in the face of the devil, receive your gift! Be filled with the Holy Spirit and speak in tongues boldly. You need it! It's a gift, and it's totally yours by faith!

PAUSE AND REFLECT. Are you operating more in the flesh than the spirit? Do you need to receive the Holy Spirit and find release in speaking in your heavenly language?

RECORD your desire for speaking in tongues and the reason why. Remember that tongues are a weapon against the enemy—Satan cannot understand or stop the flow of this communication between you and God!

ACKNOWLEDGE your need to speak in tongues continuously, knowing that the gift of tongues edifies you and imparts revelation into your soul.

YIELD yourself to Jesus. Give thanks in prayer for the empowering gift of His Holy Spirit.

6

TAKE THE OPPORTUNITY

*Thus says the Lord: "Cursed is the man who trusts in man and
makes flesh his strength, whose heart departs from the Lord.
For he shall be like a shrub in the desert, and shall not see
when good comes but shall inhabit the parched places in the
wilderness, in a salt land which is not inhabited."*
Jeremiah 17v5&6

ONE THING THAT KEEPS us vital in prayer is the responsibility that comes
with opportunities. If you want to grow in faith and in prayer with God,
simply increase your responsibilities!

As a young married couple, we were blessed with four healthy children,
all born within the space of just four years! We were young, with plenty of
energy and positive mindsets, but we knew that rather than lean on our own
limited skills, it was far more advantageous to trust God for His wisdom to
raise these children. Did we get it right all the time? Certainly not! We made
mistakes, but if there was one thing we weren't remiss in, it was covering our
children in prayer and seeking God's best for their lives. We knew God alone
was able to make up for any gaps in our parenting abilities. They needed a
Saviour, just as we did.

In our earlier years of parenting, I received the scripture above. As I read
Jeremiah chapter 17, I definitely knew which category I wanted to dwell in!
Who would choose to dwell in a parched place in the wilderness when we
could live in a place of abundance and refreshing? When we pray, we are
drawing on the refreshing water of God to nourish and nurture us, so that
we, in turn, can nurture others and prosper in the responsibilities assigned

us in life. *Prayer is acknowledging that true sustenance comes only from God.* Jeremiah 17 goes on to say:

> *Blessed is the man who trusts in the Lord, and whose hope is the Lord. For he shall be like a tree planted by the waters, which spreads out its roots by the river, and will not fear when heat comes; but its leaf will be green and will not be anxious in the year of drought, nor will cease from yielding fruit.*
> Jeremiah 17v7&8

When Bruce and I were in our late twenties, we took up the challenge to pastor a church. Bruce had attended Bible college for a short stint, which had equipped him in many areas of ministry, but we came up short in the face of the adverse spiritual realities that confronted us as we took up our role in pastoral leadership. Though zealous for the task, our understanding of the spiritual realm was lacking. We had both grown up in environments of ease, and much of our foundational faith had never been challenged.

How did we learn to handle these new realties before us? Through prayer—as every uncomfortable and challenging situation raised its head!

We can learn through all sorts of courses or manuals in anticipation of what lies ahead, but there are times we simply need to be 'out of our depth' in the responsibility entrusted to us before we truly find our footing in God. When everything remains neat and tidy, we are more inclined to unconsciously operate in our own strength. But when a situation is beyond our capabilities or frame of reference, a greater reliance is needed to draw on God through prayer. There are both problems and solutions that can only be spiritually discerned (1 Corinthians 2v14). There's a veil between this world and the next, and when we access God's presence through prayer, we are simply stepping into the invisible realm to draw on God's knowledge.

Do you have a desire to grow in your ability and develop in your place of prayer? Avail yourself of responsibility. *Step up in opportunities of service* and you will find revelation flooding your soul that you would not have possessed otherwise. How rich we are in Jesus when we respond to His call!

P AUSE AND REFLECT. Do you view your responsibilities as cumbersome chores or as opportunities to call on God for wisdom, guidance and strength?

R ECORD areas in which you could step up and take on more responsibility in order to become more dependent on God.

A CKNOWLEDGE that God is interested in every detail of your life. Invite Him through prayer to impart His wisdom and strength to your situation.

Y IELD control to God who desires to arm you with increased strength, understanding and enlarged capacity!

PART TWO
PRAYER CONNECTS

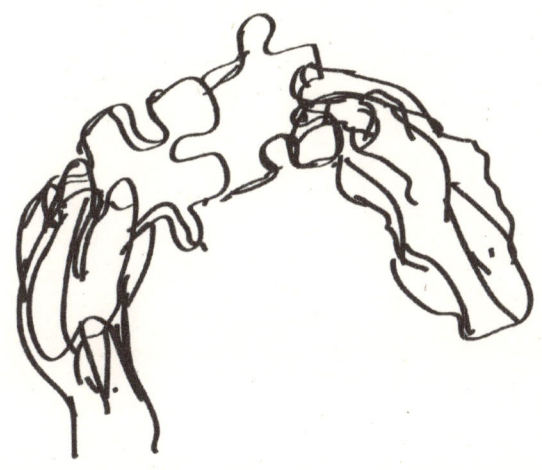

From the end of the earth I will cry to You, when my heart is overwhelmed; Lead me to the rock that is higher than I.

Psalm 61v2

7

IN THE STILLNESS

Be still and know that I am God.
Psalm 46v10

SOMETIMES WE ARE NOT able to hear God or experience true intimacy with Him because we don't know how to *be still in His presence*. How much favour do we forfeit because we take it upon ourselves to solve life's issues, offering only explanations to God and doing all the talking?

David penned Psalm 46 knowing where his strength came from when times were tough. His close relationship with God was recognisable by all who encountered him. In fact, on one occasion when King Saul was experiencing bouts of depression, a servant recommended David as one who could effectively minister to him.

> *Then one of the servants answered and said, "Look, I have*
> *seen a son of Jesse the Bethlehemite, who is skilful in playing, a*
> *mighty man of valour, a man of war, prudent in speech, and a*
> *handsome person; and the Lord is with him."*
> *1 Samuel 16v18*

Although Saul had accepted the position of king over Israel, he had not bothered to cultivate his personal relationship with God. As a result, his mental health was under serious pressure. His inability to follow God wholeheartedly rendered him vulnerable, confused, and inwardly troubled. When Saul was advised that David was a godly person who could come alongside and usher in God's presence, thus easing Saul's deep distress and torment, he welcomed the suggestion. David was a 'stand out'! In 1 Samuel 16v21 we read:

*David came to Saul and stood before him. And he loved him
greatly, and he became his armour bearer.*

Where had David developed this confident faith and sure courage? *In
the stillness.*

David's life to that point had been one of obscurity. He was simply the
youngest son of Jesse, the one who tended his sheep in the fields. But there,
in solitude during those lengthy days and nights, David constantly lifted his
heart to God, seeking Him, worshipping Him, and drawing on His closeness
and help in times of danger.

Amongst his family members, David was overlooked. He hadn't even been
considered when the prophet Samuel came on a mission to find and anoint
a new king for Israel. But David had never been overlooked by God—in fact,
God was waiting to bring David from the shadows into prominence, not only
because David's heart was fully devoted, but because he carried an anointing
for both worship *and* warfare. So it was that David was able to effectively
minister to Saul. 1 Samuel 16v23 says:

*And so it was, whenever, the spirit from God was upon Saul,
that David would take a harp and play it with his hand. Then
Saul would become refreshed and well, and the distressing spirit
would depart from him.*

David's anointing and confidence before the king came from his 'alone
time' with God, where he positioned himself to worship, pray, and commune
with His heavenly Father. When the anointing on his life became visible, it
was not through self-promotion, but by the Spirit of God. In the same way,
God wants to meet you and me 'in the stillness' in order to equip us for life
and ministry.

Are you afraid of being alone? There is an 'aloneness' that is ordained and
anointed of God where we depend on Him entirely. David came forth from
this place of 'aloneness' possessing inner strength, wisdom, and a powerful
anointing to prosper in his God-ordained position. 'Aloneness' is a choice

to simply trust in God first and foremost—a choice that ultimately stands you in a place of strength.

Does your strength and ability come from your intimacy with God, or are you dependent on the crowd for your confidence? Saul sorely lacked inner fortitude; he was totally dependent on the external environment for affirmation. David, on the other hand, carefully cultivated his relationship with God, and was recognisable as one who was filled and empowered by the Spirit of God.

P AUSE AND REFLECT. Are you drawing your strength and confidence from God, or the environment around you? Who or what is the most influential voice in your ear?

R ECORD. What changes would you need to make in order to experience being '*still*' with God?

A CKNOWLEDGE God as the only One who can grant you inner peace and the anointing to do life well. Choose to spend time 'alone' in God's presence today, praying and communing with Him.

Y IELD any need you feel to be constantly with people, and choose God first. Then watch how He will empower and position you for greatness!

8

THE HIGH PLACES

When He had sent them away, He departed to
the mountain to pray.
Mark 6v46

DURING JESUS' TIME ON earth, He often climbed a mountain to pray. Why was that? Maybe it separated Him from the commotion below, affording Him a quiet place to pray. Perhaps the connection with His Father was simply better from an elevated position!

With our need for reliable internet connection on a daily basis, Bruce and I often find we need to shift location when the reception is poor. While camping recently in a beautiful valley surrounded by hills, we found it hard to maintain a consistent signal. To reconnect to the internet, we had to go higher so our online communication could resume.

It's the same in the spirit. Sometimes we keep trying to fulfil what God has called us to, but we find ourselves overloaded, dealing with frustrations or distractions. We can even find ourselves disconnected from God. As we *ascend* in the spirit, we are able to more fully interact and engage with Jesus—we are removing ourselves from distractions intended by the enemy to interrupt our prayer life and cut the lines of communication with heaven.

The truth is, nothing can destroy the signal between us and God. Jesus never 'cuts out'! He always holds the line, awaiting our reconnection with Him, even when life's concerns have weakened the signal of faith. But we must not allow ourselves to stay grounded on a natural plane, or 'hang up' on godly hope.

In the Old Testament, the 'high places' were often elevated locations where altars had been dedicated to false gods, resulting in the establishment of idolatrous worship. Under godly leadership, many of these high places were dismantled and demolished, and as altars to the one true God were constructed in their place, true worship was restored in the nation of Israel.

It took courage for God-appointed leaders to demolish these ungodly altars. Many had been erected in honour of false gods, years before Israel's occupation. But it was important to destroy the domination they held—*and* the associated false beliefs which had formed over a long history of fear and perversion.

The enemy seeks to establish similar altars in our hearts and minds, places where we will be tempted to bow down to ungodly images and false ideals. God fully backs us and honours us, however, when we tear down idol worship and erect altars of true worship, dedicating ourselves to honouring Him. It's time to demolish strongholds of fearful thinking, false religion, and superstitions through prayerful authority, and ascend to the elevated place in the spirit where God's house has already been established.

We are to be people who *go up* to the mountain of God and to His house, that we might communicate with Him and learn from Him! It's time to deal with broken signals, disconnects, fearful thinking and occult domination. We are called to exercise godly authority and bring healing to broken bodies and conflicted minds, but this is going to take God's people ascending into God's presence in order to gain a greater perspective of His mercy and power.

What a different view we behold when we allow our spirit to be lifted before God in a *higher place* of prayer and worship!

Although we are able to connect with God anywhere and anytime, there are higher places in the Spirit of God we need to ascend to. It may require some effort on our part to connect solely with the presence of God and cut ourselves free from earthly persuasion. Let's climb to the 'high places' with Jesus today and take authority over all the enemy's power!

P AUSE AND REFLECT. Are there 'higher places' of communication with God you could access? How could you separate yourself from the 'demands of the day' to connect more deeply with Him?

R ECORD any areas of disconnect in your prayer life, and purposefully plan to spend quality time in prayer to God. From an elevated position you will gain greater perspective!

A CKNOWLEDGE God's power over the enemy. Nothing is too difficult for Him! He is simply waiting for you to connect with Him. How could you do that better?

Y IELD your excuses and feelings of powerlessness, and choose to position yourself closer to God, where the signal between you and Him is strong. Get ready for what God wants to do powerfully in and through you!

9

COME AWAY

My beloved spoke and said to me, "Rise up, my love, my fair one, and come away. For lo, the winter is past, the rain is over and gone. The flowers appear on the earth. The time of singing has come, and the voice of the turtledove is heard in our land. The fig tree puts forth their green figs, and the vines with the tender grapes give a good smell. Rise up, my love, my fair one and come away!"
Song of Songs 2v10-13

JESUS, OUR BELOVED, INVITES us to come away with Him. It is an invitation to leave a previous season and to enter into a new one. 'Coming away' may mean leaving the humdrum of everyday life to enter a moment of beautiful exchange. It may mean leaving a season of barrenness, hardship, or plain endurance, to reap a new harvest.

The turtledove's cooing call identifies that spring is coming. Around the world, spring is a season of new life, colourful displays of beauty, and renewed hope and happiness. It's a sign of a much brighter future ahead.

In this passage, the bride dreams of the bridegroom seeking her out, knocking at the door of her house, arousing and awakening her to his love. God, our beloved, desires to awaken us to His love, but unless we will *come away* with Him, we will never experience the fullness of His grace and goodness, and our souls will remain thirsty for an encounter with Him.

Without God, our hearts and souls become dehydrated. In this world we can be surrounded by magnificent beauty and amazingly brilliant people, but when there is no connection with the Creator of the universe, an internal 'withering' results—a 'thirst of the soul' occurs due to anxiety and fearful expectations. Jesus welcomes everyone who is soul thirsty to *come away* with Him. In Psalm 42 the psalmist expresses his longing in these words:

As the deer pants for the water brooks, so pants my soul for You,
O God, for the living God.
Psalm 42v1-2

Only God can satisfy the deepest longings of our soul, and unless we *come away* with Him in prayer, stillness and worship, we will continue to suffer the effects of previous seasons with a dissatisfied soul. It is therefore expedient that we *come aside* with God at regular times in order to maintain connection and communication.

We should also be ready to respond with spontaneity when God, our heavenly bridegroom, simply seeks us out. Exchanges occur during those encounters that are supernatural, life changing and defining! A word from God makes all the difference to the condition of our soul—just as it did for the Shulamite bride when her bridegroom spoke:

O my dove in the clefts of the rock, in the secret places of the cliff,
let me see your face, let me hear your voice; for your voice is
sweet, and your face is lovely.
Song of Songs 2v14

When we come into intimacy with God, there is no need to hide. Instead, we can show our true heart and form, knowing that He will encompass us with His love and approval. Until we *come away*, we will never hear the tenderness of His voice and feel the great love in His heart for us. So rise up today! He's calling you to *come away* from the worries, distractions and temptations of this world, and enjoy His presence. We are being called to draw close—so close that we can breathe His fragrance! So just 'be' in His love! These moments are not a call to war, or a call to work, but an invitation to divine exchange and revelation.

P AUSE AND REFLECT on God's invitation to *come away*, and recognise how blessed you are that your sovereign God wants to invest in your life.

R ECORD your sincere, 'thirsty-heart' prayer for revelation in these moments of encounter.

A CCEPT any inconvenience to your schedule, and simply *come away* with Him.

Y IELD your life fully to the love and leadership of the Holy Spirit.

10

CONNECTION

*So the Lord spoke to Moses face to face, as a man speaks
to his friend. And he would return to the camp, but his
servant Joshua the son of Nun, a young man, did not
depart from the tabernacle.*
Exodus 33v11

IF WE VALUE CONNECTION with God, we will spend time in His presence.
We won't view prayer as an 'optional extra' or something we *have* to do. We
will *want* to pray! To pray is to connect with God as a friend—it's like talking
on the phone to your best mate. When we connect with our friends, we stay
updated with what is happening in their world. Similarly, God wants to
keep us updated with what He is thinking and planning at any particular
moment, and to chat with us about the things He cares about.

In the Bible, Moses was described as a 'friend of God', one who God shared
with 'face to face'. In the same way, God has called us friends! He earnestly
desires connection with us, not just a relationship from a distance. Jesus said:

*No longer do I call you servants, for a servant does not know
what his master is doing; but I have called you friends, for all
things that I heard from My Father I have made known to you.*
John 15v15

If we care about God as we profess, we will *connect with Him*. This should
be our earnest desire and priority as God's chosen people.

Stop and acknowledge God daily. Make time for Jesus. Read His Word,
expecting to receive revelation from the Holy Spirit. Whatever we receive in

the way of revelation, comfort or encouragement is life-changing and will remain with us forever.

Even as a young mother with four children and endless daily tasks, I found time to spend in daily prayer and Bible reading. Some may say that with this level of responsibility, this is impossible, but because of desire I managed to *deliberately carve time out for connection* most days as it was of extreme value to me. Ecclesiastes 10v10 says, "If the ax is dull and one does not sharpen its edge, then he must use more strength, but wisdom brings success."

My aim was to accomplish the housework by mid-morning, then sit down to read the Bible prayerfully with a cup of coffee. I believe my prayer life sanctified the household to the point where our four-year-old son, who loved to sit and play at my feet, would often ask eagerly if I was doing my Bible Study. I believe my investment in prayer and reading God's Word on a daily basis released a covering of peace and calm over his life. Or maybe he was just happy because his mother was stationary for a change, and not bustling around with daily chores!

Chatting to God and allowing Him to speak into our spirits readies us for our daily activities and fortifies us for difficult seasons when they arise. It is said that a problem shared is a problem solved. This truth is even more powerful in connection with Almighty God. Sharing our lives with God in prayer transports us from natural ability to supernatural advantage in every area of life!

It is true that we need to find safe spaces and safe people to share both our joys and our needs with, wherever we are. Special exchanges of care and connection are not easily forgotten. They are empowering moments that minister to us at a deep level. But even more life-giving is our connection with God who constantly reaffirms His love, overwhelms us with His favour, and simply refuses to remember our failures.

God has life-changing words to speak to you and me, but are we connected enough to hear them? The Holy Spirit promises to bring back to remembrance every word God has already spoken into our heart when we need it. That's why it is so important to be connected. There is *an exchange in talking* with and listening to our heavenly Father. We are the benefactors of every heavenly blessing!

PAUSE AND HONESTLY ESTIMATE the level of your communication and connection with God. If you have trouble remembering what God has said to you in the past, try reading through old journals to remind yourself of the special exchanges and promises you have received.

RECORD the times in your day that you spend talking with Jesus. You may need to carve time out of your day to make it happen!

ACKNOWLEDGE that without prayer, you lack connection, and therefore are less likely to receive revelation.

YIELD your time to Him, and plan your schedule around meeting with Him. God is eagerly awaiting to impart grace into your life!

11

REFLECTIONS

As water reflects the face, so one's life reflects the heart.
Proverbs 27v19 (NIV)

EACH OF US MOST likely take time to look into the mirror every morning to ascertain whether we are presentable for the day, right? But are we as diligent about checking the condition of our heart? We need to prayerfully look into the mirror of God's Word to get an accurate reflection of how we are faring emotionally, mentally, and spiritually. Are we growing and maturing in our faith, experiencing the joy God's inner beauty brings to our everyday life?

When we read the Bible, rather than viewing it as a duty to be fulfilled, we need to ask the Holy Spirit to speak to us, encourage us, and strengthen us—but also to reflect back to us where we may fall short and where improvements could be made. The psalmist prayed:

Search me, O God, and know my heart; try me, and know
my anxieties; and see if there is any wicked way in me, and
lead me in the way everlasting.
Psalm 139v23&24

That may seem like a dangerous prayer, but it is possibly the most powerful thing we can pray, as God's revelation can save us from hurting ourselves and others.

Reflect on life's journey. This is important, not to hold us in bondage or shame, but so we can adjust and move to higher ground on our thinking, feeling and being. Reflection time is like prayerfully participating in a review to see how well we measure up to the confession of faith we profess. If we find we fall short, we can make the necessary adjustments in order to counteract any deficit God reveals. Reflecting before God is the safest (and surest) way to hear and to heal, and to ensure our ongoing wellbeing in our journey of faith.

Reflect with a desire to know Jesus better. When we pause, we may be amazed or surprised at what God shows us, but His revelation transforms our lives. We need to prayerfully behold God, gazing intently on His loveliness so we can be changed into his likeness!

But we all, with unveiled face, beholding as in a mirror the glory
of the Lord, are being transformed into the same image from
glory to glory, just as by the Spirit of the Lord.
2 Corinthians 3v18

Reflect on who you can be. This stirs desire for more of the Holy Spirit's work in our life. Prayer and reading God's Word will give us an accurate account of current reality. As we prayerfully read the Bible, the Bible reads and locates us! In life, we are surrounded with many mirrors—mirrors of culture, family, social media, peer expectation, financial success—all trying to inform us of who we are . . . or at least, who they think we should be!

The only true mirror in which we will find our identity and our purpose is in the mirror of God's Word. As we view Jesus through His Word, we more accurately discern His great love for us and the intricacy of His beautiful design for our lives individually. The more we behold Jesus, the more we will reflect who we are truly meant to be! The psalmist expressed it this way:

As for me, I will see Your face in righteousness; I shall be
satisfied when I awake in Your likeness.
Psalm 17v15

Today, let's behold Jesus. As we gaze upon Him with awe, desire will stir within us, and we will become more like Him. *How is our reflection? Can people see Jesus when they look at our life?* Spending time in God's presence enables us to reflect Jesus more powerfully. We become what we behold!

P AUSE AND CONSIDER the reflection you see in God's mirror. Is there a resemblance to your heavenly Father? Is the same goodness of your loving heavenly Father reflected through your responses?

R ECORD any painful image, or sin or hereditary iniquity from the past, that you want erased. Then look instead into God's mirror of love and purpose and write what you see there!

A CKNOWLEDGE the need daily to linger in front of God's mirror, both for encouragement and for honest assessment, praying for grace to change accordingly.

Y IELD to God's counsel, knowing He has the ultimate best look for your life.

12

POUR OUT YOUR HEART

Trust in Him at all times, pour out your heart before
Him. God is a refuge for us.
Psalm 62v8

To 'pour' literally means to dispense from one container to another, knowing the supporting vessel has the ability to handle or hold the flow. The psalmist uses this word in reference to us pouring out our heart before God, knowing that He is well able to handle our issues and help us when we need His intervention.

Pour out your heart! Many people try to simply 'box on' (as the old saying goes) in the face of adversity, but there is more wisdom in pausing, and pouring out your heart before God. David knew how to do this. In scripture we read his compositions addressing God with grief and sorrow but concluding with praise as he lifted his heart again, trusting God to intervene. As he did, God's internal peace invaded his very being.

David settled his heart through prayer. There are occasions when we just need to settle our heart by talking to God—issues that have rocked our world, hurt our hearts or confused our thinking, need to be poured out before God. Many times, we do not realise how strongly certain events have impacted our lives until we voice them before God our Father. We can 'spread' our issues before Him just as King Hezekiah did.

And Hezekiah received the letter from the hand of the
messengers, and read it; and Hezekiah went up to the house of
the Lord, and spread it before the Lord. Then Hezekiah prayed

before the Lord, and said, "O Lord God of Israel, the One who
dwells between the cherubim. You are God, You alone, of all the
kingdoms of the earth. You have made heaven and earth."
2 Kings 19v14&15

Hezekiah took the letter from the king of Assyria threatening to lay siege against the city, and spread it before the Lord. He expressed his fear and acknowledged the vulnerability he felt in person with the Lord! God spoke directly into Hezekiah's concerns and assured him of protection:

Therefore, thus says the Lord concerning the king of Assyria:
"He shall not come into this city, nor shoot an arrow there,
nor come before it with shield, nor build a siege mound
against it. By the way that he came, by the same shall he
return; and he shall not come into this city," says the Lord,
"for I will defend this city, to save it."
2 Kings 19v32-34

True to His word, the angel of the Lord took care of the problem, killing Sennacherib's entire army of 185,000 soldiers, and Sennacherib, king of Assyria, was struck down by his own sons.

Are you holding on to financial threats, family worries or health issues or are you 'spreading' these concerns before the Lord in prayer, pouring out your heart before Him? It's time to empty yourself of self-reliance and hopelessness, and totally pour out your heart before God. God is not afraid of your vulnerability, your tears, or your desperation! In fact, He is waiting to step in and avert the enemy's attack on your life. He is waiting to be invited to intervene in the issues you face!

What is currently threatening your wellbeing, your state of mind, and ultimately, your faith? What are you battling with deep inside? Despair, depression and doubt are all indicators of inner turmoil. These are common responses when personal territory is threatened by the enemy!

The best place to deal with vulnerability is at the foot of the cross, where Jesus poured out His life for ours so we could go free. Today, 'empty yourself', and pray like never before. As you pour out your heart, God will pour back into you the assurance of His presence and the power to deal with all you are facing. What an exchange!

P AUSE AND REFLECT on anything that may be seeking to threaten your health or wellbeing and your faith.

R ECORD any threat or intimidation you feel. Pour out your heart to God, spreading your concerns before Him.

A CKNOWLEDGE God's power to intervene and supernaturally turn situations around. God will do the fighting for you as you pray and rely on Him!

Y IELD afresh to God in prayer, and in return, receive His confidence, the certain expectation of better outcomes!

13

QUIETEN YOUR HEART

*In returning and rest you shall be saved; in quietness and
confidence shall be your strength.*
Isaiah 30v15

SOMETIMES THERE'S A NEED to quieten our hearts, quieten our surroundings, and just *be one with God in prayer*, listening to His voice. If the world around us becomes too loud and its concerns are amplified, we will have trouble hearing God's voice. That's why the scripture above encourages us to 'return and rest'. But return from *where*? And rest from *what*? Perhaps it is from the volume of doubt, fear, complaints and demands that constantly command our attention. In essence, we are removing ourself from any negative noise that competes for our heart causing anxiety and unbelief to dominate.

Elijah was in such a state. People and circumstances became too much for him and he felt desperate and defeated—even though he had previously witnessed God perform many amazing miracles! The sound of despondency and hopelessness had become so overwhelming that he complained vigorously, demanding that God answer him in some dramatic fashion. Such was the mood he found himself in. But God told him to go and stand on the mountain before the Lord, and then we read:

> *And behold, the Lord passed by, and a great and
> strong wind tore into the mountains and broke the
> rocks in pieces before the Lord, but the Lord was not
> in the wind; and after the wind an earthquake, but
> the Lord was not in the earthquake; and after the*

39

earthquake a fire, but the Lord was not in the fire;
and after the fire a still small voice.
1 Kings 19v11&12

There was nothing dramatic about God's response! God responded to Elijah in a quiet voice—a voice that Elijah could have easily missed, had he not been so desperate to hear. God spoke in such a manner to bring Elijah to his senses! He was not about to send down fire and smite Elijah's opposition on this occasion. Most likely, God was simply telling Elijah to calm down.

We, too, may be wanting God to answer our complaints in a dramatic fashion, only to find that He chooses to speak in a calm manner, giving directions to our heart for the exact moment we find ourselves in.

One time during our ministry, Bruce and I questioned our ability to lead and grow a church in Auckland. Despondency came knocking on the door of our hearts with the express desire to get us to quit! Bruce, however, heard the still, small voice of God while praying on a mountain near our house. He received the revelation that there was a force 'besetting us' that we needed to take authority over! If Bruce hadn't *quietened his heart* in prayer, he may have missed this important revelation. When we prayed with authority, this spirit of discouragement left, and we have never experienced the same despondency again.

Have we become hard of hearing? What volume are the distractions in our ears? And where is the mountain you can stand on and position yourself in prayer to listen to God speak? Life is busy by nature; many demands and dilemmas exist in our world, but God desires to release His calm into the midst of it all. When Elijah recognised the still, small voice of the Lord, and gave God his attention, he heard what God wanted him to do next. God reminded Elijah of his call as a prophet and the need to anoint successors before his departure from earth (1 Kings 19v15&16).

Dear reader, you are not done! Like Elijah, it's not over for you until God says it's over! There is still much to be done. God wants to whisper hope, direction and courage into your ears, but that requires *quietening your heart* to hear Him.

PAUSE AND LISTEN to the sound in your heart. Is there the sound of triumphant praise because of God's rule in your life, or is there the noise of alarm, distress, and despondency? Position yourself somewhere quiet to hear God's voice.

RECORD any changes you need to make. Bring your agenda into agreement with God, submitting yourself afresh to His voice and direction.

ACKNOWLEDGE God's reassuring presence when you come aside in prayer. Thank Him that He will speak a fresh word into your spirit.

YIELD completely to God, and experience His peace.

PART THREE
PRAYER EMBRACES

*Now hope does not disappoint, because the love of God has been
poured out in our hearts by the Holy Spirit who was given to us.*
Romans 5v5

14

LOVE PRAYS

*I do not pray for these alone, but also for those who will believe
in Me through their word: that they all may be one, as You,
Father are in Me, and I in You, that they also may be one in
Us, that the world may believe that You sent Me. And the glory
which You gave Me I have given them, that they may be one
just as We are one. I in them, and You in Me, that they may be
made perfect in one, and that the world may know that You
have sent Me, and have loved them as You have loved Me.*
John 17v20-23

JESUS' PRAYER AS HE prepared to leave earth was an earnest prayer for His
disciples to stay connected and remain one in faith and love.

If we love, we pray! Love drives us to our knees, and when we pray, our
prayers and petition reveal our love for the person, the community, or the
city we are seeking God about. Prayer is more than just asking for advice;
it's entering another realm to access God's Spirit, shutting the door on carnal
responses and helpless thinking. In prayer we avail ourselves of the person of
the Holy Spirit, the One the Bible identifies as our 'Helper'. The Holy Spirit
shows us how to pray regarding specific people and situations when we are
not sure how we should pray.

Most people worry about family members and adverse situations. Actually,
life is full of worries! But we can bring all our cares and petitions before God
with thanksgiving, eager to receive His answers. In prayer, change happens,
situations ease, and revelation invades.

Be anxious for nothing, but in everything by prayer and
supplication, with thanksgiving, let your requests be made known
to God and the peace of God, which surpasses all understanding,
will guard your hearts and minds through Christ Jesus.
Philippians 4v6&7

Let love be your motivation to pray.

Pray because you love God! When we love Him, it follows that we should be keen to communicate personally and closely with Him.

Pray because you love to see God's power at work! We need to employ diligence to seek God's will so that the sick can be healed, the disenfranchised restored, and the lost returned home. The disciples ministered in the power of the Holy Spirit because they were motivated by the love of God and 'great grace' was upon them (Acts 4).

Pray because you love people! Talk to God about the person or situation you are concerned about. Offload your concerns onto God, and allow Him to *love you back* with answers, cues, insight, and even greater revelation on how to pray more effectively!

On one occasion when burdened about one of our children, I brought the situation before God in earnest prayer. He instantly reminded me that He cared more for that child than I ever possibly could, and that I needed to hand over my concerns to Him. So right there on the beach, I yielded my burden, and as a prophetic act I gathered some sticks and composed a little altar. On that altar of wood, I laid down my desires and intentions (as good as they seemed to me), knowing that God was able to love my child more effectively than I ever could. God honoured that act, and I arose stronger from that encounter with Jesus.

Jesus was loving me as I loved another!

So, love one another by praying! Motivate yourself today to love others through the habit of prayer.

PAUSE AND CONSIDER your motivation to pray. Is it from a heart of love, or duty? What good thing may you need to lay down to receive something greater?

RECORD who you would like to love by praying for them and lifting their needs before God.

ACKNOWLEDGE that God will bring change as you love others in prayer, and that He moves as you pray.

YIELD your concerns to Jesus and expect supernatural answers to prayer!

15

BE A FRIEND

*A man who has friends must himself be friendly, but there is a
friend who sticks closer than a brother.*
Proverbs 18v24

EVERYONE APPRECIATES GOOD FRIENDS—close friends who support, reliable friends who help, and supportive friends who pick up the slack when there's a need! Jesus is the greatest friend. His Holy Spirit accompanies us everywhere we go, guiding, loving, and working on our behalf.

I see intercession in light of being a friend to those who are struggling to see breakthrough or inner desires realised. Noticing people who have been knocked down by life, I choose to come alongside them in prayer, lifting their needs before our Father in heaven.

We will never fully understand what another person may be facing until we become a 'friend in the spirit', one who is committed to upholding in prayer those who are stuck, struggling or side-lined.

The Bible relates the story of a paralysed man who was healed by Jesus simply because four committed friends persisted in getting him the help he so desperately needed! These friends knew that one encounter with Jesus was enough to change his life forever, and they worked together to make this happen. They did not just feel for their friend in his need; they literally carried him into the presence of Jesus.

*Then they came to Him, bringing a paralytic who was carried
by four men. And when they could not come near Him because
of the crowd, they uncovered the roof where He was. So when*

they had broken through, they let down the bed on which the
paralytic was lying. When Jesus saw their faith, He said to the
paralytic, "Son, your sins are forgiven you."
Mark 2v3-5

Undeterred by the obstacles, these friends didn't lose hope when accessing Jesus was difficult on account of the crowd. They persevered, creating an alternative way for the paralytic man to be brought before Jesus. Removing the tiles from the roof, they lowered their friend into the house! How innovative was that?! They broke through the restrictions, determined that God would touch their friend—and their tenacious faith gained the attention of Jesus.

Over the years I have been part of an intercession group where we view ourselves like those four friends, carrying people before the Lord for healing, release, deliverance, and salvation. We identify with the anguish of soul and paralysing hopelessness people feel, and in Jesus' name, with the heart of compassion, we reach out to assist and 'take weight' in the spirit, believing that God will intervene in their lives as we gain Jesus' attention through prayer.

To *be* a friend in this way, you first need to *know* a friend—the Holy Spirit, who directs our steps and helps us intercede and pray effectively! For the paralytic, there was more going on than his physical situation. We see this when Jesus spoke to the man, *releasing* him from sin and *freeing* him to rise from the mat of despair.

Many people are carrying heavy loads and need the assistance of those who are willing to carry them on a 'stretcher of faith' before the throne of grace. Some issues may be to do with health, finances or relationships, while other people are simply weary with battling life. They need friends with faith like you!

Are you a faith-filled friend who will take the time to pray and intercede? Are you able to break through on behalf of another? Intercession involves chipping away at the obstacles until the prayer is answered and breakthrough comes. Maybe it's time for you, along with others, to pick up a corner of a stretcher and intercede on behalf of those who are burdened and weighted down. What a joy it is to be part of someone else's breakthrough!

PAUSE AND CONSIDER. Is there someone whose load is too heavy for them to carry alone? Notice where hopelessness is dominating and determine to be a friend by earnestly seeking breakthrough for that person.

RECORD the names of those you want to bring before Jesus. In determined prayer, remove the obstacles to their breakthrough, claiming the victory and the intervention of Jesus.

ACCEPT that you have a part to play in helping others off their beds by chipping away at restrictions with faith and expectation.

YIELD time to God, making yourself available to pray and intercede. Your prayers make a difference!

16

BREATHING BUDDY

In this manner, therefore, pray: "Our Father in heaven . . ."
Matthew 6v9

SHANE WILLARD RENDERS THE opening lines of the Lord's Prayer in these words: "Our Father, in the air I breathe, I stop and become aware of You."

As Christians, faith is our natural air. The prayer of faith made on behalf of another gives that person an opportunity to inhale the oxygen of hope, whatever dilemma they are facing. We often speak of amazing things that 'take our breath away', but people's breath can also be restricted because of negative or harmful situations. Panic can cause the airways to tighten, restricting the flow of oxygen and subsequently leaving a person gasping for air. Prayer and petition by the people of God can bring an ease, a relaxing of the tension associated with the issue at hand.

People might become breathless during exercise or exertion, but afterwards, the heart slows its beating and regulates the breathing back to a normal rate. When this doesn't happen, intervention is necessary. Likewise, when stress and strain are left unaddressed, it has a detrimental effect on our spiritual, emotional and mental health. I see prayer as intervention between the person and the problem, releasing the capacity to 'breathe easier', enabling them to grasp the truth of God's Word and to quiet their heart by recollecting His specific promises.

I have experienced such grace in situations when people have committed to pray for me behind the scenes—in fact, I have witnessed God's power released into my very breath! What does this mean then? It means we need our spiritual lungs to be filled with the air of faith. Without it, our spiritual lungs lose their capacity to believe, and can even collapse. It is a frightening experience to have one's lungs collapse. In these situations, artificial equipment is required to assist the breathing process—external intervention is needed for breath to become regulated and the heart to recover its equilibrium.

So, stop and pray! Don't just battle on your own or leave others to battle on their own. In scuba diving, there is a rescue technique used in 'out of gas' emergencies. In this situation, divers have a buddy who will share their mouthpiece (or demand valve) if one person gets into trouble. By alternatively breathing from the gas source, both the diver in trouble and their 'buddy diver' are generally able to ascend to the surface and recover.

I visualise myself as a *breathing buddy*, praying for others in their difficulties until they can breathe freely again for themselves. Knowing I have enough air in my faith tank, I am able to share my spiritual oxygen mask with others until they recover. Lots of situations in life can cause people to feel out of their depth, gasping for breath. Prayer can make all the difference in assisting them to breathe, surface and survive!

How about you? Perhaps you need to ascertain where your breathing has become laboured. What circumstance, doubt or lie has taken your breath away? Today, breathe in the Holy Spirit for yourself. Allow Him to fill your spiritual lungs with truth and hope-filled expectation. Allow God, your breathing buddy, to come alongside and release extra oxygen in the form of dreams and vision into the chamber of your heart. Then witness every tightness dissipate in His presence. Breathe in God's delight over your life, and through prayer become a 'breathing buddy' for someone else on their journey.

P AUSE AND RECOGNISE where you or others may be running low on
spiritual oxygen, or where the tank of faith has become empty.

R ECORD areas where you may be running low in faith and in capacity
to cope, and draw on the breath of God to help you. Breathe
in His Word and His presence as you refill and refuel in prayer.

A CTIVATE! Share your faith with others, knowing that your prayers enable them to breathe easier. As you share your oxygen mask of faith, know that others will be rescued, resuscitated and revived.

Y IELD your breath to God, and find the infilling of faith and vision.

17

PRAYER COVERS

*Surely He shall deliver you from the snare of the fowler and
from the perilous pestilence. He shall cover you with His
feathers, and under His wings you shall take refuge; His truth
shall be your shield and buckler.*
Psalm 91v3&4

AREN'T YOU GLAD THAT God covers you, protects you, and delivers you
from danger by sheltering you under His wings? We also need to protect
and keep others safe by covering them with prayer and spiritual authority.
When we are given responsibilities, whether physical or spiritual, God calls
us 'gatekeepers', people who are prudent about what can be let into our
environments, and what should remain without.

There is power in protective, watchful prayer. In the Old Testament we
read of watchmen who literally sat on the walls of a city, discerning both
good and negative influences. Prayer is our elevated position! Unless we
are praying, we may be ignorant of the enemy infiltrating, taking advantage
of people, and destroying godly purpose. By prayerfully watching over the
areas we are entrusted with, we can identify areas of potential weakness and
discern any force that may be seeking unlawful entry through those gaps. We
live in a spiritual world where enemy forces seek to prey on people's hearts
and minds. Let's cover our areas of responsibility with prayer! Let's not take
things for granted.

Here are some areas we can cover in prayer:

Households and children. As a young mum with children at home, I
knew I was positioned as a 'watchman' for my household. I covered my home

with prayer, discerning any force that sought to invade and come against my children's lives. As an overseer of my household, I had the authority to protect my family from harmful, deceptive spirits. I could outwit the enemy! I covered my children in prayer as they slept, as they went to school, and as they engaged in their many activities. At the same time, I could release blessings and call out the creative will of God in their lives.

Work places. As Christians, we are strategically positioned by God to change atmospheres and release blessings and God's favour over our colleagues and employees. Our work space should be better because we are there as a believer!

Spiritual leadership. We are to cover those we lead with prayer and protection. However, if we are to provide a covering for others, we need to also come under covering! Don't take spiritual covering for granted—it's a powerful principle ordained by God. Rise up and bless those who stand in a position of caring for your soul. The Bible says:

> *Obey those who rule over you, and be submissive, for they watch*
> *out for your souls, as those who must give account. Let them do so*
> *with joy and not with grief, for that would be unprofitable for you.*
> *Hebrews 13v17*

Bruce and I have been blessed as we have allowed others—namely, the eldership of our local church and the national leadership team of our movement—to oversee and cover us in prayer. Sadly, those who resist accountability are 'uncovered' and therefore more vulnerable to enemy attack.

Nehemiah provides a great example of covering the people in prayer. As the returned exiles rebuilt Jerusalem, Nehemiah remained on the wall where he took responsibility for dealing with the enemy, thus protecting the people from attack. From the height of the wall, Nehemiah could discern any intimidation, resistance and mocking spirits that sought entry. He simply dismissed requests that did not warrant his attention and dealt with opposition, fending off dangers and sparing the workers from having to interact with demonic forces (Nehemiah 6v3).

Let's keep our environments spiritually safe and healthy through our intentional prayers of covering.

PAUSE AND REFLECT on your areas of responsibility. How well are you covering those you are entrusted with in prayer?

RECORD specific times to pray for covering for those you love against every distraction the enemy sends to distract and derail them.

ACKNOWLEDGE and call out the specific areas where God desires to bless and prosper those under your responsibility. Speak out their God-given destiny in prayer!

YIELD yourself to spiritual covering and instruction, so you may be a good example to those you are responsible for.

18

PRAYER WATCHES

I wait for the Lord, my soul waits, and in His word I do hope.
My soul waits for the Lord more than those who watch for the
morning—yes, more than those who watch for the morning.
Psalm 130v5&6

PRAYER IS THE EXPRESSION we give to our faith and God-given vision. In response to faith, we lift our head, and watch and wait, expecting to see God answer these prayers.

Anna and Simeon waited with anticipation in their hearts to see answers to the prayers they had prayed. Anna was a prophetess, a godly woman who was looking for the redemption of Israel and had directed her prayers accordingly. In Luke 2v36-38 we read:

> *Now there was one, Anna, a prophetess, the daughter of*
> *Phanuel, of the tribe of Asher . . . who did not depart from*
> *the temple, but served God with fastings and prayers night*
> *and day. And coming in that instant she gave thanks to*
> *the Lord, and spoke of Him to all those who looked for*
> *redemption in Israel.*

Anna recognised Jesus from the moment she entered the temple that particular day. Because Anna had prayed over a long period of time, her spirit knew exactly who she was looking for. The Holy Spirit bore witness in her heart that this was the Messiah she had awaited! *Prayer enables us to recognise the answer when it comes.*

What can we learn from Anna?

Anna did not depart from the temple. She remained faithful in her service to the Lord and was in constant pursuit of God's purpose through prayer. Prayer is an investment into the future God has planned. How many people, through impatience, desert the place of prayer, becoming dismissive of God's house and discounting His very presence and power to heal instead of staying at their post and pushing through in faith! When we vacillate, we can miss the powerful redemptive answer to our prayer.

Anna was alert in the Spirit. She didn't waver in unbelief but held hope in her heart for the redemption of the nation of Israel. That is why Anna saw not just a baby being brought to the temple for dedication, but the Saviour of the world, the much-awaited Redeemer.

Another person who watched and waited for Jesus' arrival was Simeon. Having been prophetically advised, Simeon's arrival at the temple coincided with baby Jesus' visit.

> *And it had been revealed to him by the Holy Spirit that he would not see death before he had seen the Lord's Christ. So he came by the Spirit into the temple. And when the parents brought in the Child Jesus, to do for Him according to the custom of the law, he took Him up in his arms and blessed God and said: "Lord, now You are letting Your servant depart in peace, According to Your word; For my eyes have seen Your salvation . . ."*
> Luke 2v26-30

We need to be watching, discerning the season, and recognising what the Spirit of God is doing at any point of time, just as Anna and Simeon did. Our spirits need to be awake, watchful and discerning, especially during 'night' seasons which may seem lengthy and difficult. Let's make sure we don't discard our post in prayer!

PRAY AND WATCH for the light of God to break through, even if it currently seems dark and hopeless.

RECORD your prayers and the answers that come, recognising that God's timing is always perfect. Determine to stay present and watchful, knowing Jesus will breakthrough on your behalf!

ACKNOWLEDGE the grace of God to sustain you through waiting seasons and keep you alert to the movements of God.

YIELD your demands for God to answer when you see fit. Trust Him for the right timing. He is faithful!

19

EMBRACE WISDOM

Your ears shall hear a word behind you, saying, "This is the
way, walk in it," whenever you turn to the right hand or
whenever you turn to the left.
Isaiah 30v21

OVER MY LIFETIME, GOD has released direct words into my spirit to pray and meditate on whenever we have approached new seasons of growth and responsibility. These specific scriptures become a point of meditation, stirring faith and belief within to apprehend these truths as a reality in my walk with God.

Words from the distant past that I prayed long over in faith have now become permanent beliefs in my way of operating. Ephesians 6v10 is one of them: "Be strong in the Lord and in the power of His might." Another is from Romans 8v11:

But if the Spirit of Him who raised Jesus from the dead dwells
in you, He who raised Christ from the dead will also give life to
your mortal bodies through His Spirit who dwells in you.

These scriptures are just two of the many God has prompted me to apprehend by faith—not just on an intellectual level, but on a deeply spiritual basis. They highlighted the need to shift from being an overly responsible person to someone who knew how to operate fully in the power of God. Where human power falls short, God's power goes beyond!

Recently while revisiting a season of ministry, God whispered another directive in my ear through my daily reading. You see, prayer should often take its lead from scriptures which He 'quickens' to our heart.

Through reading Proverbs 4v8: "Exalt her (wisdom) and she will promote you. She will bring you honour when you embrace her", God spoke to me about *embracing wisdom* in the coming season of my life. Wisdom has the power to promote me and accelerate the work of God both within and through my life. To 'embrace' something simply means to bring it close to your heart, just as a parent would a newborn child! So the exhortation of this scripture to me personally was to draw God's wisdom close while entering the new season.

Proverbs 4 also speaks about the security of wisdom. Wisdom brings calm within, aiding and assisting us in our walk. Proverbs 14v33 says, "Wisdom *rests* in the heart of him who has understanding."

There are also directive scriptures, such as Proverbs 4v11,12: "I have taught you in the way of wisdom. I have led you in right paths. When you walk, your steps will not be hindered and when you run you will not stumble." Finding God's wisdom helps me succeed in my endeavours and eliminates how many times I stumble. In the natural, and at any age, we cannot afford to fall physically, as we may break bones and do serious damage!

The same applies in the spirit. When embarking on new ventures, we want to walk with the security, ease and strength of God's wisdom accompanying us. If we entertain carnal pathways, there is the danger of tripping, breaking our spirit, losing our confidence, and possibly costing us relationships.

We have a choice to figure out life for ourselves or to tap into the wisdom of God. As I have drawn from God's wisdom, I have experienced more divine leading, supernatural energy, breakthroughs, and desired growth than ever anticipated. God is so good like that!

What directive scripture motivates you to pray in your current season? What is the passage of faith you are claiming and integrating into your life? We never go past needing a specific word from God for the season we are in. These directives give us the 'how to' and the confidence in executing the will of God.

I am fully convinced that God directs our believing by creating new opportunities and having us seek Him in prayer for what we need. How vital and exciting is the function of God's Word to propel us forward into His prosperity!

P AUSE AND IDENTIFY specific scriptures that God has been highlighting to you, and start praying them into being. Experience them as a growing reality within.

R ECORD these seeds of scripture that will prove powerful in bringing change within your heart and circumstances.

A CCEPT the season God has for you, knowing He wants to help you by directing your prayer.

Y OU ARE GOD'S CATALYST, and His Word within you will accomplish more than you could possibly believe!

PART FOUR
PRAYER TRIUMPHS

Through God we will do valiantly, for it is He who shall
tread down our enemies.
Psalm 108v13

20

COMMISSIONING ANGELS

*No evil shall befall you, nor shall any plague come near
your dwelling; For He shall give His angels charge over you,
to keep you in all your ways. In their hands they shall bear
you up, lest you dash your foot against a stone. You shall
tread upon the lion and the cobra, the young lion and the
serpents you shall trample underfoot.*
Psalm 91v10-13

WHAT AN AMAZING PROMISE! God commissions His angels on our behalf
to rescue us from dangerous or difficult predicaments. Angels will aid us,
strengthen us, and preserve our lives in the face of evil opposition. We may
be surprised to realise that angels are with us constantly.

*Those who trust in the Lord are like Mount Zion, which
cannot be moved, but abides forever. As the mountains
surround Jerusalem, so the Lord surrounds His people from
this time forth and forever.*
Psalm 125v1&2

How wonderful and comforting to know we are surrounded by the Lord
and His angels. As God's children we have the authority to commission angels,
acknowledging their presence and their ability to safekeep our family, our
community, and the things that are dear to our hearts.

When our church purchased the Mercury Theatre in Auckland in 1994, I
prayed specifically for God's angels to surround the building, stationing them
to guard and protect 'our going in and coming out'. Located in the red-light

district, I was aware of the spiritually unsavoury area in which the theatre was situated. My prayer and declaration became, *"This is a house of truth, and nothing with evil intent can enter this building."* By forbidding entry to any deceptive or contrary spirit, a guard was set over our building, ensuring safety throughout the life of the church.

Where do you need to commission angels to work on your behalf? Is any evil intent or plan of the enemy seeking entry, spreading fear in your heart or home, or disrupting your place of worship?

Maybe you are facing ongoing sickness or financial woes. The enemy seeks to force entry, but God's angelic hosts are well-able to withstand any attempt. Like tall, strong bodyguards, angels deflect danger and keep safe those who belong to Christ.

Bruce and I experienced an angel assisting us when we were in South Africa. In the form of an ordinary man, he beckoned to us, warning us of danger in the location we were in. He then led us safely back to a bus depot where we quickly returned to Johannesburg. We hadn't realised we were in an unsafe place—we were just doing the 'tourist thing'—but we believe to this day that God provided and commissioned security in the form of an angel.

Safely back at our hotel, we heard about the recent murders of tourists in that particular location. We were so grateful that heavenly bodyguards always heed His voice and are ready to take charge at God's bidding (Psalm 103v21&22).

Scripture again and again speaks of *angel armies* that defeated the enemy on behalf of Israel and various individuals, causing the enemy to flee. These angel armies surround us and protect us also. Let us be aware of their presence and acknowledge the protection they afford us.

God sometimes sends angels in the form of everyday people for another purpose—to encourage and strengthen us. Our hospitable reception allows God's messengers to speak significantly into our lives.

> *Do not forget to entertain strangers, for by so doing some have*
> *unwittingly entertained angels.*
> *Hebrews 13v2*

Let's commission angels today to safeguard all that concerns us and to assist us in our warfare against the enemy. Let's also receive the messengers God sends to encourage and strengthen us on our journey.

PAUSE AND REFLECT on God's hand over your life. How has He already preserved and rescued you from dangers and troubles?

RECORD any present troubles that warrant the commissioning of angels to guard and keep you. Give thanks for the constant presence of God's angels around you.

ACKNOWLEDGE the presence of angels, not only to fight, protect and provide for you, but to direct, encourage and strengthen you.

YIELD yourself to God and station His angels around every concern and difficulty you face.

21

BINDING AND LOOSING

*Simon Peter answered and said, "You are the Christ, the Son
of the living God." Jesus answered and said to him, "Blessed are
you, Simon Bar-Jonah, for flesh and blood has not revealed this
to you, but My Father who is in heaven.*
Matthew 16v16-17

PETER'S CONVICTION OF WHO Jesus was did not come from his own mind
but was a revelation of truth from above. In response to this, Jesus bestowed
authority on Peter to operate at a higher level of spiritual influence, saying,

*"You are Peter, and on this rock I will build My church, and the
gates of Hades shall not prevail against it. And I will give you
the keys of the kingdom of heaven, and whatever you bind on
earth will be bound in heaven, and whatever you loose on earth
will be loosed in heaven."*
Matthew 16v18&19

We can exercise true godly authority over demonic forces only according
to the revelation of truth received, not according to our preferred philosophies
and ideals. Truth endows us with an inner godly authority. Scripture declares
that when we know the truth, the truth sets us free. Scripture also tells us that
man's wisdom is foolishness in God's sight and carries no weight or authority
to bring about any change within the heart of another.

The New Testament qualifications for those in church leadership include
holding to sound doctrine and having a commitment to the authority of
God's Word. The same is also required of every Christian, enabling us to

exercise spiritual authority so that lives and environments can thrive and prosper. There is a 'flourishing' that occurs when our lives and affairs are placed under the governance of God and His Word.

Here's a thought: Would Jesus endorse *your* statements of faith like He did Peter's? Would Jesus put His weight behind *your* claims? Soundness of faith based on God's truth releases authority to bind and loose using the keys of the kingdom according to His will.

What may need 'binding' in your situation? Is there anything operating outside the will of God, opposing your wellbeing and impairing or weakening your faith? When human wisdom prevails, self-seeking exists on many levels, and displays of unhelpful behaviours such as greed, anger and control will manifest. In these situations, the enemy gains a foothold in our lives. We need to exercise authority and bind the spiritual force that is in operation.

To 'bind' means to 'tie together; make fast or tight as with a rope or band; hold or restrain as if tied or tied down; or gird or encircle with a belt' It literally means to stop any movement and activity.

Are you aware of any activity that is causing you to fear, or experience limitation in any way? Expose this intimidation by identifying and naming the spirit that is sabotaging your confidence, your health, and your relationships. Take authority, binding it in Jesus' name. In other words, declare it no longer has permission to operate or have any form of control in your life. Speak out loud, "In the name of Jesus, I bind that spirit of (for example, manipulation) over my life and forbid it to operate any longer!"

To 'loose' means to set something free. We loose the kingdom of heaven over our own lives, the lives of others and over environments, by releasing the love and peace of God though prayer. Just as we use keys to unlock doors in the natural, we possess spiritual keys that release the blessing of God.

When Jesus was on earth, He took authority over the domination of the enemy in people's lives. He subsequently gave us the same authority to bind demonic activity and release divine blessing. Spiritual discernment will help us identify what is in operation and what spiritual keys are necessary to bring release and relief to situations. Jesus always addressed issues and took authority over demonic powers that were present. This ushered in His kingdom, causing lives to flourish and His purposes to be fulfilled. We need to speak to the issue at hand, bind the enemy's activity, and by speaking out loud, release the blessing in Jesus' name.

P AUSE AND RECOGNISE any spiritual force that may be bearing down on you or your loved ones that needs to be bound and broken in the name of Jesus.

R ECORD the activity that needs to cease and the subsequent victory that needs to be experienced, knowing that all authority has been given to you to pray in this manner.

A CKNOWLEDGE the power that is contained in the truth of God's Word and speak it out boldly over situations and people.

Y IELD afresh to the Spirit of God and determine to sharpen up in spiritual wisdom and discernment!

22

GROANING

Likewise the Spirit also helps in our weaknesses. For we do not know what we should pray for as we ought, but the Spirit Himself makes intercession for us with groanings which cannot be uttered.
Romans 8v26

WE GROAN WHEN WE feel intense pain or distress, especially when we don't have the ability to address or fix the situation at hand. Groaning deep in our spirit occurs when we are unable to find the words to express the severity of the pain or the enormity of the need. It is a sign that things are not as they should be—that something is seriously out of order, and that we long for God's help in the challenge before us.

We also who have the firstfruits of the Spirit, even we ourselves, groan within ourselves, eagerly waiting for the adoption, the redemption of our body.
Romans 8v23

While on earth, Jesus 'groaned' in His spirit over many situations, expressing empathy and sorrow. Just after Mary and Martha had lost their brother, we read that Jesus "groaned in the spirit and was troubled" (John 11v33).

Jesus understood that Lazarus was about to be raised from the dead, but the sisters were yet to grasp the reality of the resurrection power of Jesus. Godly groans are an expression of our deepest longing for God to take over in any troubling situation. Our groan is a sign of our utter helplessness and total inability to remedy or correct the problem in our own strength—it's a raw expression of our total dependence on Jesus.

Are you groaning today? What situations do you need God to step into? What intense desires lie deep within that overwhelm you and render you speechless? The Spirit of God can translate your 'unspoken groaning' and turn it into effective communication before the throne of God.

> *Now He who searches the hearts knows what the mind of*
> *the Spirit is, because He makes intercession for the saints*
> *according to the will of God.*
> *Romans 8v27*

How comforting to know that God hears and understands the cry of our heart. Waiting for answers can be stressful and all-consuming, but we can be confident in God's timing. The breakthrough and the delivery of the promise *will* take place just as He promised! The Message version puts it like this:

> *The moment we get tired in the waiting, God's Spirit is right*
> *alongside helping us along. If we don't know how or what to pray,*
> *it doesn't matter. He does our praying in and for us, making*
> *prayer out of our wordless sighs, our aching groans. He knows us*
> *far better than we know ourselves, knows our pregnant condition,*
> *and keeps us present before God. That's why we can be so sure*
> *that every detail in our lives of love for God is worked into*
> *something good.*
> *Romans 8v26-28 (MSG)*

Be encouraged today that whatever concerns you, God has it covered! Every situation simply awaits the perfect timing of His delivery. God understands your groaning and affirms the deep longings expressed by your spirit. He understands the wordless sighs and the growing pains. He is faithful to support you and answer your prayers.

PRAY with passion from your spirit. God understands your heart's cry even in the absence of words. Don't be discouraged that you can't articulate as you would like to.

RECORD any groaning or agony in your spirit that needs to be brought before God, knowing that Jesus can interpret your longing and will bring it on your behalf before the throne of God.

AFFIRM and thank God for His help and care in every distressing situation.

YIELD to God afresh in faith, knowing that Jesus can handle every difficulty with ease and is releasing His peace over you.

23

—

AUTHORITY

Submit to God. Resist the devil and he will flee from you.
James 4v7

To EXERCISE AUTHORITY IN the supernatural realm and resist the devil, we need to first be submitted to the ultimate authority of God and His Word. Humility cures worldliness—any way of thinking that is self-centred, self-seeking or self-glorifying. When we place ourselves under God's rule, however, we can rise with godly authority.

That's where prayer comes in. *Prayer is a place of submission before God.* It is where we submit our thoughts, will and decisions, and commit ourselves to His Word and His will for our lives.

God is forever transforming our minds. We only see in part, but the Holy Spirit will reveal more of the mind of God as we surrender and come aside to seek His face in prayer. In the words of 1 Corinthians 2:9-11,

> *". . . eye has not seen, nor ear heard, nor have entered into the heart of man the things which God has prepared for those who love Him." But God has revealed them to us through His Spirit. For the Spirit searches all things, yes, the deep things of God. For what man knows the things of a man except the spirit of the man which is in him? Even so no one knows the things of God except the Spirit of God.*

We need to be 'in the spirit' to apprehend the fuller picture of God's plan and comprehend what He has already prepared for us. Too often, people want God to defer to their choices rather than letting go of control and listening to His voice. These people may wonder why their prayers are not answered. It is because prayer is where we listen and embrace the will of God. That's where true authority is born, the place where our hearts are positioned for what God has endorsed.

Personally, I can testify that any authority I carry has come from a place of intimacy. I am only able to know God's will for my life through prayer and meditation—simply listening, hearing, and being confident in the revelation He has entrusted to me. In this way, God reveals His plans to my safe keeping, entrusting me to faithfully outwork them according to His design. I then simply follow in obedience. That's where true authority comes from; it carries the knowledge and confidence that God will back me because I am not insisting on my own way but following His direction. Much joy and fruitfulness has come to my life through the directives God has revealed. His directives always work out and produce what He intended!

Paul attests to this also as he faithfully outworked the call of God on his life. We read:

> *"According to the grace of God which was given*
> *to me, as a wise master builder, I have laid the*
> *foundation, and another builds on it."*
> *1 Corinthians 3v10*

How did Paul get the authority to call himself a 'wise master builder'? He was able to speak this way because of the grace that operated through him in building churches and raising leaders.

Paul, who had previously operated from a place of harsh rule, control and domination, submitted to God's grace following a powerful encounter with Jesus. Grace then enabled him to bear fruit for God's glory and accomplish what he was unable to do through the law. Law brought bondage, but grace brought ease and an anointing of strength. Paul no longer put confidence in his own ability but in the power of God to defy the enemy and bring about kingdom purposes. This is why Paul often bid farewell to the saints with salutations of grace—he knew that's where true power and blessings lay.

How can we know what God's authority looks like in our lives? Let's start by discerning the God-given grace we are in possession of. When we come in prayer with a hunger to serve God, we will be able to fully apprehend His grace, and as a result, operate in His authority.

P AUSE AND REFLECT on where the grace of God shows up in your life. As you seek God, the Holy Spirit will bear witness to where God has granted you His authority.

R ECORD the specific call and grace God has granted you and prepare to flow and operate in His authority by giving yourself to prayer.

A CKNOWLEDGE that 'greater grace' is available to those who humble themselves and submit to God. Who wouldn't want empowering grace to help them achieve, prosper, and influence their world for Christ?!

Y IELD completely to God's plan. Welcome His authority in your life, and witness His plans being gloriously outworked by His power.

24

FORGIVE OTHERS

". . . forgive us our debts, as we forgive our debtors."
Matthew 6v12

IN PRAYER WE NEED to seek pardon for our own wrongdoing, but we also need to extend forgiveness to those who have hurt or offended us, releasing them from our judgment. This opens us up to the healing power of God to free us from any pain, anger and frustration.

Though our feelings may be justifiable in certain circumstances, we have no right to *hold onto them*. It is impossible to experience freedom within while we are harbouring unforgiveness toward another. Holding a grudge or vendetta places pressure on our emotions, creating obstacles in our journey of faith and draining us of vitality. Make it a regular habit to let go of resentment by voicing forgiveness toward another, either alone before God or in the company of a mature believer. In the words of James 5v16: "Confess your trespasses to one another, and pray for one another, that you may be healed."

Extending forgiveness toward others sets us free. Why would we want to 'limp' through life when we can 'soar' instead? Let's recognise unforgiveness for what it truly is.

Unforgiveness is a trap of the enemy to bind us and restrict our growth.

Unforgiveness breaks our spirit. It locks us in a prison of mental and emotional torment, occupying far too much space in our thinking and feelings, and crowding out the Word of God.

Unforgiveness gives permission for bitterness to spread. Bitterness defiles our mind and heart, and ultimately affects our physical body. The Psalmist wrote:

When I kept silent, my bones grew old, through my groaning
all the day long . . . My vitality was turned into the drought of
summer.
Psalm 32v3&4

Unforgiveness shuts heaven over our lives. It cuts us off from the flow of God's blessing toward us by limiting our ability to receive.

A brother offended is harder to win than a strong city, and
contentions are like the bars of a castle.
Proverbs 18v19

Unforgiveness yokes us to our own bitter judgments. We will struggle to advance in certain areas if we hold strong judgements against others.

Judge not, that you be not judged. For with what judgment
you judge you will be judged; and with the measure you use,
it will be measured back to you.
Matthew 7v1&2

Unforgiveness has been likened to drinking poison and hoping the other person dies. The poison of unforgiveness affects personal lives, families, and organisations, impacting generations to come. This is why Hebrews 12v15 warns us to look carefully, ". . . lest any root of bitterness springing up cause trouble, and by this many become defiled."

How do we know if we are harbouring unforgiveness? By looking at the conversation in our hearts and lives. What are we consistently talking about? Are we thinking ill of others or being overly condemning and judgmental? Is there an unnatural curiosity about the activities of another? Are we constantly blaming others for our state while making excuses for any negative behaviour on our part?

We need to change the conversation of our heart and talk to God instead, acknowledging any unforgiveness, knowing that He can lift the heavy weight from our shoulders. He can break the oppressive prison we may have found ourselves confined to. God grants us the ability to forgive and let go of every grievance so we can experience true freedom. When we 'voice' our forgiveness before God the Father, He releases us from the heavy labour that unforgiveness brings to our lives.

Our great example is Jesus, who released forgiveness to those who had betrayed him as He hung on the cross. He cried, "Father, forgive them, for they do not know what they do" (Luke 23v34). Jesus' desire was to ascend into the presence of His Father in heaven with a pure heart, having accomplished forgiveness of sin for all who believe.

Let's choose today the freedom God offers through extending the grace of forgiveness.

P AUSE AND REFLECT whether any unforgiveness or resentment may be residing in your heart.

R ECORD any bitterness you detect that has the power to impair your heart, health, and prosperity. Make it a regular habit to voice forgiveness toward others who may have hurt or offended you. Speak it out before God and, where necessary, in the presence of another believer.

A CKNOWLEDGE the value of freedom is a pure heart and a sincere faith.

Y IELD to Jesus and follow His wonderful example.

25

FORGIVE YOURSELF

There is therefore now no condemnation to those who are in Christ Jesus, who do not walk according to the flesh, but according to the Spirit.
Romans 8v1

IN FORGIVING OTHERS, WE release them from our judgment. In forgiving *ourselves*, we release any judgment we harbour toward ourselves.

Could you be holding yourself prisoner to past words and deeds? Are you still lamenting or regretting certain events where godly standards were breached? Condemnation brings heaviness to our hearts. If you are grieving over past events or wishing you had responded differently, you may need to 'call time' on the condemnation.

Condemnation is a robber. It pilfers the valuable time we need to process mistakes in a healthy manner. Condemnation is like a rope around us, limiting our freedom to explore and express ourselves freely. If condemnation fills our heart, it will restrict our responses, shut down our faith, and strangle any initiatives that God may be prompting us to respond to.

Condemnation is a killer of dreams. The devil knows he can flatten us by constantly reminding us of past offences and failures and reinforcing feelings of unworthiness. Have we become the enemy's best ally, unwittingly assisting him by condemning ourselves? Any sense of self-condemnation within us makes the enemy's job a whole lot easier in persuading us away from faith and obedience.

Condemnation is a suppressor of hope. It makes the future look bleak and miserable. Condemnation seeks to dull the 'why' (purpose) behind the 'what' (mission) by causing us to hesitate in our response to faith ventures or by bringing collapse and betrayal when we step out in faith, therefore confirming our deepest fears. Many missional ventures are sabotaged through condemnation and insecurity.

Condemnation is just a feeling. Yes, it relates to past facts, but it doesn't need to be our permanent state of mind. Condemnation will yield when resisted, when we submit instead to the power and the authority of the blood of Jesus. It is not our destination! God fully forgives us when we confess our sins, so we in turn forgive ourselves and release all condemnation. We need to recognise the taunts of condemnation quickly and disarm its origin, forbidding it permission to feature in our life.

Today, name self-condemnation for what it is—a robber, a killer of dreams, a suppressor of truth, and nothing more than an inaccurate, unhelpful feeling. Time waits for no one, so let's not dwell on failures from the past but learn from them and grow beyond them. We need to stop living in regret. When we speak words of forgiveness toward ourselves, we can live more fully in the present and move more confidently into the future. We cannot wait for our feelings to come fully into alignment, but by faith we need to forgive and release ourselves from any condemnation and judgment. Faith is *agreeing with God*, and in God's sight our faith is more pleasing than any sacrifice to try and make amends. Beating ourselves up or striving is not God-glorifying as it doesn't acknowledge that He was the perfect sacrifice who dealt completely with the penalty of our sin. David agreed with God when he wrote:

> *The Lord will perfect that which concerns me; Your mercy, O Lord, endures forever; do not forsake the works of Your hands.*
> Psalm 138v8

Are you feeling burdened about something God has already released you from? Are you striving to *do* better instead of *receiving* the most perfect and powerful sacrifice? Release yourself today in prayer from past mistakes, guilt, and condemnation.

P RAY AND REFLECT. Are any clouds of condemnation looming over your life and your thinking?

R ECORD every condemning thought and seek God's full forgiveness. Then forgive yourself for past failures and regret. Stop punishing yourself and replaying mistakes in your mind. Instead, speak out forgiveness toward yourself.

A CKNOWLEDGE God's power to release you in the present and restore confident hope for the future.

Y IELD to God's sanctifying presence and allow Him to release you into freedom.

26

SHOUT TO GOD

Clap your hands, all you peoples! Shout to
God with the voice of triumph!
Psalm 47v1

WHEN WE ARE GOING through a trial, the last thing we may feel like doing is *raising our voices* and proclaiming God's victory. But that is exactly what we need to do if we are to acknowledge God and silence the enemy. In the face of fear, we can declare the victory Jesus has already purchased for us on the cross. Faith-filled declarations can pull us out of any doubt-filled or despondent place we may be trapped in.

Many times during Israel's history, the enemy was defeated through the praise of God's people as they exalted His name. Have you ever sung yourself into freedom? Songs that magnify Jesus have the power to transform us at the deepest level as we passionately give voice to who He is. Let's decide today to open our mouth and shout to God with the voice of triumph! The Psalmist exhorts us with these words:

On your feet now—applaud God! Bring a gift of laughter. Sing
yourselves into his presence!
Psalm 100v1&2 (MSG)

How comforting to experience the presence of God with us even in our times of testing. God is constantly working on our behalf. Let's choose to give voice to a song of victory not only in public settings but also in our private devotional life, knowing that God always leads us in triumph!

*Now thanks be to God who always leads us in triumph in Christ,
and through us diffuses the fragrance of His knowledge in every
place. For we are to God the fragrance of Christ among those
who are being saved and among those who are perishing.*
2 Corinthians 2v14&15

If we are feeling constantly defeated or despondent, this is not of the Lord. As Christians we may go through difficult seasons, but at the same time we can be confident that God is still leading us into triumph. We 'win it' first on the inside even if the outward reality seems to indicate the contrary.

Triumph refers to a great victory or achievement. The processional entry of a victorious general into ancient Rome depicted a moment of triumph. Likewise, when Jesus rode into Jerusalem on a donkey, the people, in unison with heaven, gave testimony to who He truly is. In that moment, the enemy's voice was silenced. Praise opens the heavens!

What victorious parade of God's triumph is evident in your life? Does the fragrance of your Saviour diffuse through you, revealing His majesty and power? In prayer, let's reinforce and declare boldly the victory we have in Christ. Pray from the side of victory, remembering that nothing that has happened to date, nor anything that is to come, can separate you from God's love and power.

*Who shall separate us from the love of Christ? . . . we are more
than conquerors through Him who loved us. For I am persuaded
that neither death nor life, nor angels nor principalities nor powers,
nor things present nor things to come, nor height nor depth, nor
any other created thing, shall be able to separate us from the love
of God which is in Christ Jesus our Lord.*
Romans 8v35-39

The Greek word for 'conqueror', *hypernikaó*, means 'to go over the top' of opposition to possess what Christ has already promised. It's easy for us to get discouraged amongst the difficulties of life, but instead of accepting defeat, let's meditate on all we have overcome in Christ already, and raise a voice of praise and give a victory shout to God. That is the victory that is worth shouting about!

PAUSE AND REFLECT. Is there a sound of victory in your prayer life? Or do your prayers sound more like lamentation and petition?

RECORD your declarations of faith and prophetic triumph. God loves to hear your confidence in His ability to deliver and set free. Raise up a shout of praise to Him and sing your way into His victorious presence!

ACCEPT that you don't need to *feel* victorious before you declare your victory! Speak out boldly, and your feelings will come into line with hope, faith, and confidence.

YIELD yourself afresh to Christ and His victory on the cross. This is where the ultimate victory for you was won!

27

TESTIMONIES TALK

Your testimonies are also my delight and my counsellors.
Psalm 119v24

DID YOU KNOW THAT our testimonies can speak to us? This is why it is important when we approach God in prayer to consider what He has already done in our life.

Testimonies counsel us—bringing our hearts back to a place of faith, especially if our minds are prone to wander or we feel overwhelmed with our current situation.

Testimonies help us deal with doubt—the sense of fear and timidity which so often raises its head in the presence of both opportunity and challenge. So let your testimonies talk to you. Let them build you up in faith when you lack courage and strength, or when you feel diminished in any way.

Hear my cry, O God; attend to my prayer. From the end of the
earth I will cry to You, when my heart is overwhelmed; lead me
to the rock that is higher than I.
Psalm 61v1&2

Testimonies help us remember—that God has come through for us before, and He will come through again! He is an 'again God'!

Testimonies magnify the faithfulness of God in the past, assuring us of His presence and power for the future. This is one reason why the Bible is so relevant; it is full of testimonies—accounts of significant breakthroughs in the lives of ordinary people who found the power and strength of Jesus to possess God's promises to them.

Through meditation on testimony we can muster fresh courage and vision to continue our walk. Much counsel tells us to reduce, scale back or diminish our expectations, but faith in God enables us to level up and step out, shifting our trust away from our own ability, and onto the promises God has spoken.

I believe God wants to awaken faith in our generation to counteract every demonic spirit of complacency that seeks to lull believers into settling for 'just getting by'. Recalling personal testimonies of God's help in the past has enabled me to maintain forward momentum in my walk with Him. Meditating on supernatural breakthrough over fear, deliverances from hereditary iniquities, and physical healings, has helped me remain focussed with faith and tenacity on the future. Likewise, recalling significant prophetic words and scriptures God has given me builds my faith for the 'much more' in God in the future.

The people who know their God shall be strong, and
carry out great exploits.
Daniel 11v32

When I pray, I ask God's testimonies to speak to me. God has called us to do extraordinary things to bring glory and honour to Him in our lifetime. Let's not shy away because of present difficulties but press through, knowing we stand on a firm foundation of testimonies.

Whenever Bruce and I inadvertently get separated, Bruce will use a low-key whistle which I am familiar with to help me locate him, even in a large crowd of people or a vast shopping mall. God, as our Shepherd, 'whistles' into any spaces of lostness, confusion or bereavement we might be experiencing, calling us back to the remembrance of who He is and what He has done. Testimonies speak to us—they echo within and help us stand strong.

Pause today and thank God for His work in your life thus far. Gratitude gets us going again on God's *freeway of faith*! Take a look at these scriptures from Psalm 119 in The Message version:

Guide me down the road of your commandments;
I love traveling this freeway!

I set your instructions to music and sing them
as I walk this pilgrim way.

My troubles turned out all for the best – they
forced me to learn from your textbook.

Your commands give me an edge on my enemies; they never
become obsolete. I've even become smarter than my teachers
since I've pondered and absorbed your counsel.

By your words I can see where I am going; they throw a
beam of light on my dark path.
Psalm 119v33, 54, 71, 97-98, 105

If you have ever travelled on winding roads for some distance, you may, like myself, express a sigh of relief when you reach the freeway and can travel more freely with less concerted effort. Let's not live burdened, laden down with heavy weights, but travel God's freeway of faith with joy and confident expectation. Let's draw strength from our past testimonies, mediate on them, and let them lead us into a place of ease.

P AUSE AND REFLECT on testimonies of when God came through for you. Recall times of significant breakthrough and provision and thank God for His goodness.

R ECORD your desire for future breakthroughs. Prayerfully meditate on testimonies in God's Word that align with God's counsel for your life.

A CKNOWLEDGE God's abiding presence to locate and stabilise you.

Y IELD afresh to God. Leave the winding roads of doubt and begin to joyfully ride God's freeway of faith!

28

STEALTH

*A wise man scales the city of the mighty, and brings
down the trusted stronghold.*
Proverbs 21v22

PRAYER IS A TRAINING ground where we discern strongholds that keep
individuals, communities and cities locked in fear. Atmospheres need to
be overcome, and the great news is, we are able to do this, pulling down
strongholds through the faith and authority we have in Jesus Christ. It takes
stealth and skill to 'scale a city' that looks formidable and is tightly secured,
but the Holy Spirit imparts strength and agility as we seek God's strategies
in prayer.

What strongholds in your life need to be pulled down in Jesus' name?
Many people reside in oppressive atmospheres, yet they are too fearful to
challenge the spirit behind it. When atmospheres have existed for very lengthy
periods, hopeless resignation toward the atmosphere can prevail. People put
up with a discouraging environment simply because it's familiar. We need to
challenge false allegiances, false comforts, and false beliefs. Why would we
want to miss out on God's best because of complacency and apathy?

As we wait on God, He will give insight and strategies to accomplish
seemingly impossible tasks. Just like Spiderman, the imaginary superhero
who not only climbs the face of high buildings with ease, but leaps between
skyscrapers in his mission to rescue victims and defeat the enemy, we need
to come *over and above* these strongholds in prayer, ascending to the heights
in God as we exercise His authority.

The lust for money, power, esteem and approval are examples of strongholds that influence people's decisions and actions, restricting the flow of God's grace and freedom. Such idols will always fall short in delivering on what they promise. Fear is another stronghold that needs to be demolished and brought down.

Prayer can go where we can't. We destroy strongholds by prophesying the will of God into situations, declaring God's vision for cities, communities, and individuals. Scripture tells us that it is righteousness that exalts a nation, not man-made structures. Ungodly edifices will crumble and fall when truth and faith in Jesus are declared.

Today, picture yourself scaling the heights. Imagine yourself like Spiderman leaping from building to building with ease, or like a rock climber who scales great heights by securing a pickaxe firmly into the side of the mountain and rising higher and higher step by step. Remember, God alone can give us the strength and ability to climb 'over and above' and take authority over demonic strongholds.

> *He makes my feet like the feet of deer, and sets me on my*
> *high places. He teaches my hands to make war, so that my*
> *arms can bend a bow of bronze. You have also given me the*
> *shield of Your salvation; Your right hand has held me up,*
> *Your gentleness has made me great. You enlarged my path*
> *under me, so my feet did not slip.*
> *Psalm 18v33-36*

This scripture has been of huge personal encouragement to me, guaranteeing me the agility to scale heights and the tenacity to hold on, even when underfoot platforms appear narrow and insecure. By faith God enables me to walk in places I would naturally shy away from. When my heart falters, this passage reminds me that He has given me the feet of a deer, not only to stand on narrow, difficult places, but *to bound over opposition and spring over divides and abysses.* This has been my experience as I have stayed in prayer and faith. We have a choice to make, either to stay encased by difficulties or to operate with authority at new heights.

Look around and acknowledge what you observe. Do you see people, families, communities and cities in bondage because of man-made and demonic structures? What are the towering issues? Is there pride, sickness, discouragement, depression? If so, trust God to broaden the ground under your feet, secure your foothold, and strengthen your grip. It's time to 'scale the city' and bring those 'trusted' strongholds down!

P AUSE AND OBSERVE. What towers above and intimidates you or the community you reside in?

R ECORD structures built from pride and human ambition. Recognise that only God can meet the felt need of people's hearts.

A CKNOWLEDGE that in the Spirit you have agility and skill to scale faulty strongholds in prayer and bring them down.

Y IELD to truth and righteousness, and prophesy God's Word to edify and build.

PART FIVE
PRAYER PROMPTS

I will stand my watch and set myself on the rampart,
and watch to see what He will say to me, and what I will
answer when I am corrected.
Habakkuk 2v1

29

EVERYDAY THANK-YOU'S

*Enter into His gates with thanksgiving, and into His
courts with praise. Be thankful to Him and bless His
name. For the Lord is good; His mercy is everlasting,
and His truth endures to all generations.*
Psalm 100v4&5

THANKFULNESS IS AN ATTRIBUTE that can be easily overlooked or viewed as an 'added extra' in the hustle and bustle of life. But thankfulness carries so many benefits. It opens the gates to higher, supernatural realms, lifting us beyond the 'here and now'. Our expression of thanksgiving and praise is the password into God's presence! It also contributes greatly to our wellbeing and progress.

A thankful heart is a happy heart. When gratitude lives in our heart, joy resides there too. You rarely see people who express thankfulness displaying a grumpy disposition. Gratitude squeezes out negativity. Thankfulness introduces us to a world of faith, limitless possibilities, and powerful opportunities in God. When we choose to highlight God's goodness and our belief in His care for us, negativity no longer has the power to frame our world.

A thankful heart is attractive. People respond to expressions of appreciation. Hearts are opened wider when we show gratitude and gestures of thankfulness.

A thankful heart releases heavenly peace. Jesus welcomes heartfelt praise and gratitude for who He is, and in return, smiles with favour on our lives. Philippians 4v6&7 says, "Be anxious for nothing, but in everything by prayer and supplication, with thanksgiving, let your requests be made known to God; and the peace of God, which surpasses all understanding, will guard your hearts and minds through Christ Jesus."

A thankful heart gives us an audience with Jesus. This is best displayed in the story of the ten lepers:

> *And one of them, when he saw that he was healed, returned,*
> *and with a loud voice glorified God, and fell down on his*
> *face at His feet, giving Him thanks . . . So Jesus answered*
> *and said, "Were there not ten cleansed? But where are the*
> *nine? Were there not any found who returned to give glory*
> *to God except this foreigner?" And He said to him, "Arise,*
> *go your way. Your faith has made you well."*
> Luke 17v15-19

A huge miracle had taken place in ten people's lives—these people had been delivered from the cruel affliction of leprosy with all its social and natural limitations. They had been released from a literal prison. Ten lepers were healed by Jesus but only one returned to thank Him. We sense grief in Jesus that nine of them failed to recognise and glorify God for His intervention. The one who returned to say 'thank you' received an extra word from Jesus.

Thankfulness guarantees a welcome and provides a way forward with His help! Let's bring our gratitude to God in prayer. Here are some everyday thank-you's we can express:

Gratitude for creation. How beautiful is this world that God has created?

Gratitude for salvation. Without Jesus we were condemned to death, but through His blood shed for us, our sins are completely forgiven and cancelled.

Gratitude for the sanctifying work of the Holy Spirit which transforms us from the inside out, equipping us to live an overcoming life.

Gratitude for everyday blessings such as food, provision, housing, family, good health.

Gratitude for work, our purpose and mission. We get to do the works of God—how amazing!

Gratitude for family and friends.

Gratitude for those who lead us and champion us in our Christian walk.

Gratitude for the Word of God. What a privilege that He speaks to us and that we can communicate freely with Jesus at any time.

How about starting your day by entering His presence with joy and thanksgiving? Thankfulness grants you access to the very throne room of your heavenly King and opens the heavens over your life!

PAUSE AND REFLECT on the level of gratitude that you speak out to Jesus.

RECORD your daily blessings and thank Him in prayer. This releases God's presence and power over you.

ACKNOWLEDGE that it is impossible to fulfil God's will in your life without Him, and thank Him for His help!

YIELD all negativity, doom and gloom. Light up your world with daily thanksgiving.

30

HEAVEN KNOWS

*But you, when you pray, go into your room, and when you have
shut your door, pray to your Father who is in the secret place;
and your Father who sees in secret will reward you openly.*
Matthew 6v6

HEAVEN KNOWS! PEOPLE USE this old saying when they feel at a loss to know
what to do next or when they don't know how a situation will unfold. At least
in this somewhat glib expression there is an underlying acknowledgment of
a higher entity—a belief that perhaps heaven can handle the complexities
and knows what is happening.

We can take great comfort in the fact that heaven *does* know! Heaven
sees, hears, and recognises the genuine investment of prayer that we make in
bringing His kingdom to earth and witnessing His healing and restoration
work in people's lives. It is easy to just shrug our shoulders in the face of a
complexity, but when we pray, we are placing our issues and burdens in God's
hands, acknowledging our lack and expressing confidence in His ability to
outwork the solutions.

Heaven sees. Maybe you feel unseen or insignificant in the overall scheme
of things, when in fact you are seen by your heavenly Father who loves you.
Jesus saw the reality behind the widow's offering:

> *He looked up and saw the rich putting their gifts into the*
> *treasury, and He saw also a certain poor widow putting*
> *in two mites. So He said, "Truly I say to you that this poor*
> *widow has put in more than all; for all these out of their*

abundance have put in offerings for God, but she out of her
poverty put in all the livelihood that she had."
Luke 21v1-4

Jesus was moved by the sacrifice of this poor woman. He perceived her heart of faith and trust. Likewise, He sees and hears every petition, every request, every prayer of faith.

Heaven knows the people who are truly moving mountains by faith, subduing kingdoms, and ruling and reigning with Christ. In fact, we may be surprised in the final analysis who receives the accolade, "Well done good and faithful servant." It may not be the ones we assumed were the most obvious.

Heaven knows, heaven sees, and heaven hears!

So keep praying! Keep lifting your voice in prayer, both in private as well as in public. Give little thought to who may notice you or whether you will receive honour for your diligence. Prayer and the offering of our time and resources is like creating a building in the invisible realm. The investment is not seen at first, but eventually that which has been sown in the unseen realm becomes visible in the natural realm.

Heaven knows and records every sacrifice of prayer made on behalf of others, for cities, for countries and nations. We can be confident that heaven knows when we pray, and we can trust God for the right outcome. Through prayer, we can tackle matters well beyond our capability, believing God will surprise us with breakthroughs in unexpected ways. Heaven acknowledges you and God leans in to hear the cry of your heart, so keep meeting with Jesus, keep committing those difficult areas to Him, and watch how He will work on your behalf!

P AUSE AND REFLECT on your investment of prayer into the concerns of life. Do you release complexities heavenward to Jesus, or do you simply muddle along in the chaos?

R ECORD your worries, unresolved matters, desires, and any long-held vision. Continue to sow in the Spirit, knowing that God stands ready to answer.

A RRANGE a time and a place to 'offload' in prayer knowing that you have an audience of One who listens intently to your heart's cry.

Y IELD the weight of your concerns to Jesus and rejoice in the knowledge that *heaven knows, hears, sees, and will respond accordingly.*

31

SUBTITLES

Call to Me, and I will answer you, and show you great and
mighty things which you do not know.
Jeremiah 33v3

NOW IN OUR SEVENTIES, Bruce and I have discovered that we don't always hear accurately and we miss sentences in movies and programmes on television. It is reassuring to know that at the press of a button we can bring up subtitles on the screen. This guarantees a much more pleasurable viewing experience!

God loves to show us the big picture of His mission—but like a movie playing out before us, we often need to ask for 'subtitles'—we need to enquire further about the things we haven't heard or quite understood correctly. God will always reveal the 'subtitles' when we seek Him!

Samuel was to be a prophet to the nation of Israel, and scripture tells us that 'none of his words fell to the ground'. What Samuel declared came to pass! We read:

Now the Lord came and stood and called as at other
times, "Samuel! Samuel!" And Samuel answered, "Speak,
for Your servant hears." Then the Lord said to Samuel:
"Behold, I will do something in Israel at which both ears
of everyone who hears it will tingle."
1 Samuel 3v10&11

God had been revealing His big picture to Samuel, but when Samuel enquired further, God gave him more detail. Samuel sought God for the 'subtitles'—for greater understanding of the words he was to deliver. God is willing to break it down for us so we can better comprehend how to build and serve the vision entrusted to us. Many proclaim boldly that they are 'big picture' people yet fail to build anything lasting or impacting. Why is that? Is it because they fail to perceive the steps that are needed to fulfil the bigger plan of God? *Don't miss the subtitles!*

> *Blessed is the man who listens to me, watching daily at my gates,*
> *waiting at the posts of my doors.*
> Proverbs 8v34

Many people want to 'put the roof on the vision' before establishing the framework. God establishes the framework that allows us to build toward the fulfilment of the vision. Are we enquiring of God regarding the 'how to'? Are we watching and waiting for directions? Sure, we can find operating instructions in manuals and teaching material, but it is more important to hear a word from God and implement it.

Subtitles are often displayed in prophetic words. At one point in our ministry, Bruce and I had a vision to plant a church in London. We perceived that this church would be a 'beachhead' from which many other churches would be planted across Europe. But within that larger vision there were many subtitles, one of them being the importance of 'hospitality'. God spoke this specific word to us from Proverbs 9:

> *Lady Wisdom goes to town, stands in a prominent place,*
> *and invites everyone within sound of her voice: "Are you*
> *confused about life, don't know what's going on? Come*
> *with me, oh come, have dinner with me! I've prepared a*
> *wonderful spread—fresh-baked bread, roast lamb, carefully*
> *selected wines. Leave your impoverished confusion and live!*
> *Walk up the street to a life with meaning."*
> Proverbs 9v3-6 (MSG)

As a result of adhering to this small but strongly emphasised 'prophetic subtitle' about the importance of hospitality, the London church flourished, indeed becoming a 'beachhead' that branched out and launched ministries and churches throughout Europe. Prophetic words ensured the 'framework' was in place for God to build upon. We have found that listening to God in prayer for the 'subtitles' has guaranteed success in many endeavours.

God has big vision for all of us, but as lofty as a vision may seem, listening in prayer enables us to fine-tune the steps needed to build a framework which will support that vision. You may have a vision for a wonderful marriage, but unless you comprehend the subtitles on how to build a good marriage, you may find your vision imploding rather than being established. Let's be faithful to take the small steps that we hear in the spirit. God is so faithful to speak. Let's discover the details in the subtitles as we tune in to His voice.

P AUSE AND REFLECT on the big picture God has given you. Recognise the fine print—what are the steps associated with achieving it?

R ECORD your ability as a reader of God's subtitles. Could you improve in this matter? What is God highlighting to you?

A CCEPT that you are not skilful enough to build something lasting on your own unless you read God's instruction manual. What steps have you missed?

Y IELD to the Holy Spirit and ask God to fill in the necessary details.

32

CALENDAR PRAYER

*Teach us to number our days, that we may
gain a heart of wisdom.*
Psalm 90v12

Do you use a calendar to remind you of birthdays, meetings, or social outings? Bruce and I usually note special events in our diaries. We don't want to miss important occasions because we haven't planned for them. We can also use our calendars to prompt prayer, providing timely reminders to pray for certain individuals on certain days. I have a calendar in our bathroom that prompts me to pray for the specific family member whose name appears on that day. Having a notification in front of me is a great stimulus to intercede for that person. In that way, all of our family members get covered by prayer. Of course, we can pray whenever they come to mind, but a calendar can help us develop a more regular habit of prayer.

This was the strategy of the praying wife in the film, 'The War Room'. This woman covered her closet walls with post-it notes filled with words, declarations, and destinies that needed to be contended for in prayer. Her prayers proved powerful in shifting obstacles in the spirit and releasing breakthrough for others. Concentrated prayer works wonders in dealing with difficult and obstinate barriers. It is helpful to highlight and target specific needs for prayerful attention using a visual aid like a calendar, especially when consistent spiritual warfare and intercession are necessary.

We can also set up our calendar to remind us to pray blessing and covering over family members and friends, that they would become recipients of God's grace, love, and power. Young lives are particularly susceptible to the spirit of the age, and we can cover and protect them through our prayers. Have you ever sensed that someone has prayed consistently for you? Perhaps you have literally experienced the strength and empowerment of their prayers? As a young mother, I prayed many specific prayers for my children. This is one I regularly declared:

> *All your children shall be taught by the Lord, and great*
> *shall be the peace of your children.*
> Isaiah 54v13

How awesome it is to see a full prayer-calendar! Each name represents a person who carries dreams, desires, and aspirations. As we rise in a systematic manner to pray for others, the might of God is awakened within hearts to understand and grab hold of God's will and purpose for lives—He wants to 'wake up the mighty men'!

> *Proclaim this among the nations: "Prepare for war!*
> *Wake up the mighty men, let all the men of war draw*
> *near, let them come up."*
> Joel 3v9

Prayer helps safeguard and direct lives into the fullness of God's best. Heaven waits to pour out God's great blessings upon the lives of those we love.

Prayer prompts prophecy—we can declare in faith what we sense God has spoken!

Prayer doesn't take a huge amount of time. Short prayers in response to a calendar prompt help in a powerful and positive way to release the anointing of God.

There are always rewards and joy from investing in people's lives through prayer. Today, get your calendar out and allocate daily space to pray for others. Who is on your prayer list? Commit to pray for others in a more systematic way with prompts that will keep you focused and committed. Your prayers make a difference, and lives will be greatly enriched and blessed by your diligence.

P AUSE AND REFLECT. How consistent are you in praying for the people in your world? Do you want to up your game? Would calendar entries assist in this process?

R ECORD a list of names and needs in your calendar to uphold and support regularly in prayer. Prayer does make a difference!

A CKNOWLEDGE the support in prayer you have received from others. Acknowledge too God's power to intervene; He is not limited by physical distance but can touch lives as we pray.

Y IELD your time to God and incorporate regular, meaningful prayer into your daily schedule, taking on responsibility to intercede and warfare for the benefit of another.

33

PRAY A PSALM

*All Scripture is given by inspiration of God, and is profitable
for doctrine, for reproof, for correction, for instruction in
righteousness, that the man of God may be complete, thoroughly
equipped for every good work.*
2 Timothy 3v16&17

SCRIPTURE IS VITAL FOR our Christian growth. Many people fail to realise
the power that is contained in the written Word of God, especially when
activated under the anointing of the Spirit of God. What better way to
learn and implement scripture than to pray the word—especially scriptures
that God underscores. If you are not sure how to pray, hold your Bible in
your hand and begin by praying a Psalm out loud. Try using Psalm 65 as a
prayer-prompt:

A prompt to give thanks (v4):

*Blessed is the man You choose, and cause to approach You, that
he may dwell in Your courts. We shall be satisfied with the
goodness of Your house, of Your holy temple.*

This verse can become an expression from our lips, thanking God that
He has chosen us. You might say, "Thank You, God, that You have chosen
me and that I can approach You at any time. Today I choose to dwell with
You and experience the fullness and goodness of Your love." As you speak out
with thanksgiving, this truth will lodge in your spirit more fully and destroy
any intimidation from the enemy.

A prompt to express how great God is (v5,8):

By awesome deeds in righteousness You will answer us,
O God of our salvation. You who are the confidence of
all the ends of the earth . . . You make the outgoings of
the morning and evening rejoice.

God longs to show His awesomeness through His deeds in response to our declaration of faith and confident expectation that He will not only answer our requests but go well 'above and beyond' our hopes.

A prompt for those struggling with impossible situations (v5-8):

All your salvation wonders are on display in your trophy
room. Earth-Tamer, Ocean-Pourer, Mountain-Maker,
Hill-Dresser, Muzzler of sea storm and wave crash, of
mobs in noisy riot—Far and wide they'll come to a stop,
they'll stare in awe, in wonder. Dawn and dusk take
turns calling, "Come and worship." (MSG)

We may be praying for people who are experiencing financial hardships, health challenges, or overwhelming threats of loss. Let's use the scriptures to speak out our faith in response to the greatness of God, who has the ultimate say in every situation. When we read the verses and declare them aloud, our confidence grows in the certainty of God's intervention. As God moves in supernatural power this will draw others to worship too.

A prompt to acknowledge God's provision (v9-10):

You visit the earth and water it, You greatly enrich it; the river
of God is full of water; You provide their grain, for so You have
prepared it. You water its ridges abundantly, You settle its
furrows; You make it soft with showers, You bless its growth.

As we use these words to acknowledge God's faithfulness in sustaining and providing for us, the Holy Spirit will continue to awaken our spirit to the fullness of His presence. He will heighten our sensitivity to His outpouring and release growth in areas of previous drought and discouragement.

A prompt to declare God's favour (v11-13):

> *You crown the year with Your goodness, and Your paths*
> *drip with abundance. They drop on the pastures of the*
> *wilderness, and the little hills rejoice on every side. The*
> *pastures are clothed with flocks; the valleys also are*
> *covered with grain; They shout for joy, they also sing.*

Let's agree with God for His favour, releasing joy and celebration over every new year.

PREPARE to pray by opening the scriptures. Choose a Psalm and declare God's promises contained in the passage. Start there and watch how the Holy Spirit will unpack further truth as you pray.

RECORD the words of a Psalm that will strengthen your faith. Declare it, believing that God will answer your needs with awesome deeds. Nothing is too difficult nor out of His reach.

ARTICULATE God's Word by praying scripture out loud. Spoken truth has power!

YIELD to God and allow the prompting of Psalms to lead you into more powerful times of prayer.

34

CUES AND CLUES

Then He came to the house of the ruler of the synagogue and
saw a tumult and those who wept and wailed loudly. When
He came in, He said to them, "Why make this commotion and
weep? The child is not dead but sleeping."
Mark 5v38&39

How did Jesus know this little girl hadn't really died? All the evidence pointed to the fact that she was dead.

Jesus had a cue—He knew in His spirit that He was about to awaken her (and the surrounding crowds) to His power.

Do we recognise the leading of the Holy Spirit, prompting us to pray for events and people? Think of the times when people simply 'come to mind'. Maybe it's someone we have not seen for a while, but now they are in our thoughts and sometimes our dreams. Don't miss these moments to follow through in prayer. We may not know what that person is going through, but God is calling us to intercede on their behalf, nonetheless. I have found that I no sooner think about someone, than I either hear from them or hear some news regarding them. On other occasions I have had a clear dream about a person that has caused me to immediately intercede for them.

I was once prompted in a dream regarding a certain young woman whose life, God showed me, was under threat. I began to pray, and I involved others also. Sure enough, four months later that same young woman, in another part of the world, was suddenly subjected to a life-threatening illness. She was not expected to recover, and yet over the months following, she recovered miraculously. Committed prayer on our part, in response to a prompting, had intercepted this severe attack on her health.

How is God prompting you? Is there someone or some situation He is placing on your heart? Will you stop and lift your voice in prayer before Him? *Cues and clues* in God are not that difficult to hear or recognise, but let's watch that busyness doesn't cause us to be dismissive or neglectful of these promptings.

A vital aspect of our spirit is intuition. When filled with the Holy Spirit we can pick up clues that are essential for our own wellbeing, and the wellbeing of others. We can also discern spiritual forces that may be working in situations.

A vital element in prayer is faith, not fear. An acquaintance of ours had only been given a one percent chance of recovery, but God quickened us to pray in a certain way. We were to take a strong stance of faith, positioning this woman firmly on the other side of the cross where God revealed that He had already healed her. Did she look like she was healed? Not at all. Although every organ was shutting down and she was on life support, we weren't deterred from praying as directed. We responded to God's cue, and little by little this woman recovered from an incredibly intense attack on her health. How effective prayer is when we follow the lead of God!

What should we do when prompted? Stop immediately and pray in the Spirit! Claim a promise fitting for the need, one quickened by the Holy Spirit. *Make that promise your prayer.* Stay in faith, knowing that God is working. Trust Him for a supernatural outcome.

God wants to 'sharpen' our ability in the Spirit, but if we are non-responsive to His voice He will simply move onto someone else who is quick to hear and quick to respond. God is speaking to us far more than we realise. We must not think that promptings are just our own thoughts and fail to lift people in prayer before God. We will be so much more effective in prayer when we follow the *cues and clues of the Holy Spirit.*

P AUSE AND REFLECT on occasions when God has sought your attention. How did you respond? What supernatural breakthrough came as a result?

R ECORD the prompts and intuitive thoughts God sends your way. He is constantly seeking your attention, desiring to work miracles, perform healings and bring breakthroughs in response to your prayers.

A CKNOWLEDGE and repent of any apathy in responding to God's voice.

Y OKE YOURSELF to Jesus and tune in to the voice of the Holy Spirit in your everyday walk with God. Your prayers matter!

35

PRACTICAL TOOLS

*But you, when you pray, go into your room, and when you have
shut your door, pray to your Father who is in the secret place;
and your Father who sees you in secret will reward you openly.*
Matthew 6v6

THERE IS NO DOUBT that a rich relationship is reserved for those who prioritise their connection with God. Prayer involves setting specific time aside to chat with God. As in any relationship, quality time needs to be planned if there is to be genuine connection and deep satisfaction within that relationship.

God longs to interact with us and reveal things we would never have understood with our natural minds. Here are a few practical tools to assist you:

1. Go into your 'room'

Identify the space that works best for you, allowing you to connect with God in a meaningful way. If this seems impossible, take encouragement from Susanna Wesley, wife of busy London pastor, Samuel Wesley, and mother of nineteen children. Susanna was a remarkable woman. She schooled her children at home for six hours a day and gave each child one hour of quality time per week, ensuring they were growing in their faith. Even with such a large family, Susanna committed herself to prayer for two hours every day. In her situation, there was nowhere quiet to retreat to. Instead, she created space for personal communion with Jesus by sitting down and flipping her apron over her head. The children learned that this was her *set apart time*, taking care of each other while Susanna spent time with Jesus. Two of her offspring became prominent Christian leaders in England later in life—John

Wesley initiated a nationwide revival, changing the course of English history, and Charles wrote approximately nine thousand hymns, some of which we still sing today.

What a legacy is forged in prayer! Prayer is doing the work that honours and touches the heart of God. In prayer, problems are solved, worlds are changed, and faith is born. When we consider Susanna's wonderful example, what excuse do we have not to spend time in prayer?!

2. Shut the door on distractions

Prayer can be a challenge for some folk—not knowing how to pray, where to start, or how to focus. But prayer is simply an interaction with just you and God. For some people, worship music can help create a beautiful atmosphere in prayer. However you 'shut the door' on distractions, know that God will meet you there.

3. Pray to your Father

Address your prayer to your heavenly Father, knowing that He is committed to care and provide for you.

4. Set a timer

In my earlier years, I found my mind tended to bounce here and there even though I tried to concentrate in prayer. It helped me to set the timer on my phone, allocating certain minutes to different people or needs and recording in my journal what God said as I prayed. If we aim too high or are too lofty in our expectation of our personal prayer life, we can be tempted to give it away when we fail to reach our goals. Setting the timer for three, four or five minutes at a time helped me focus on my prayers and stay in the designated 'lane' until the alarm rang. I found that a more effective prayer life sprang forth from this habit as God guided my voice in intercession more directly because of my focus.

Are you lamenting that you cannot pray for long, or that your prayer life is difficult? Just like any other strengthening exercise, 'prayer muscle' is built by small bursts of practice. When we allocate three minutes to five different topics for example, we have effectively prayed consistently for fifteen minutes. Maybe this method doesn't seem very 'spiritual', and the timer sounding may be somewhat annoying, but if this is what it takes to develop muscle and conversational time with God then it is worth doing.

5. Translate your thoughts into prayers

Chat with God, sharing your thoughts with Him. In turn, you will gauge His heart for certain people and subjects.

Let's go to prayer, using whatever practical tools we can to help us connect with the heart of God!

P RAYER is doing the work of faith! Talking doesn't affect change. Calling on God's intervention and exercising your faith through prayer is what makes the difference!

R ecord the consistent prayers that you are committed to pray. Keep yourself on track if you need to, by setting the timer.

A CKNOWLEDGE that prayer gives you clear direction, strengthens your conviction, and releases confidence that God will send the answer!

Y IELD your time to God and create space to pray. *It pays to pray.*

36

SHAPE YOUR PRAYERS

*Don't fret or worry. Instead of worrying, pray. Let petitions
and praises shape your worries into prayers, letting God
know your concerns. Before you know it, a sense of God's
wholeness, everything coming together for good will come
and settle you down. It's wonderful what happens when
Christ displaces worry at the centre of your life.*
Philippians 4v6&7 (MSG)

PRAYER LIBERATES US AND keeps us in shape spiritually. Everyday
distractions seek to pull us out of shape with God's perfect plan. Prayer
keeps us spiritually fit and adaptable to God's pattern—it 'suits us and serves
us' to live our best life. Why would we compromise God's pattern and yield
to anything other than His perfect plan for our lives?

In his letter to the Corinthians, Paul exhorts the church to stay on track
and in faith by implementing certain disciplines. This includes the discipline
of prayer, which is the only way to cultivate our relationship with God and
understand His heart for us. Paul writes:

*I discipline my body and bring it into subjection, lest, when I have
preached to others, I myself should become disqualified . . . All
things are lawful for me, but not all things are helpful; all things
are lawful for me, but not all things edify.*
1 Corinthians 9v27 & 10v23

Prayer trains us to stay focused. No one knew this better than Paul. He
would not permit himself to preach to others unless he was in good shape

himself. To be naturally fit, we need to train. This involves stretching our capacity beyond our comfort levels to attain the flexibility and agility we desire. It is the same in the spirit. We need to exercise the spiritual disciplines of prayer, faith, and obedience—even when it is inconvenient or we feel 'time poor'. Perhaps we need to take a look at our daily decisions and determine if they are enhancing God's perfect plan, or if certain choices are causing us to become spiritually flabby, sloppy in our responses, and lacking the vitality that epitomises a genuine Spirit-filled life. Regular prayer helps us stay in faith, stay fit, and stay focused on God's best.

Prayer gauges our spiritual fitness. When we use equipment in a gym, we are able to gauge our physical strength and capacity to withstand pressure. Similarly, our participation in daily prayer helps us monitor our responses and reactions on a spiritual level. Prayer reveals how strong we are at resisting evil. It will also show us if we may be harbouring idols or tolerating foolishness in our heart. The Holy Spirit will always blow the whistle if we are offside His eternal plan for our lives.

And the peace of God, which surpasses all understanding, will
guard your hearts and minds through Christ Jesus.
Philippians 4v7

Prayer realigns us, giving opportunity for the Holy Spirit to speak into problem areas in our life. This will help redirect our prayer and our disciplines to line up with God's desire. Alignment is key to settling our spirits and seeing prayers answered.

Prayer trains us in discernment, and we become quicker in combating contrary spiritual forces. We recognise the nature of what may be seeking to cross our path.

He teaches my hands to make war, so that my
arms can bend a bow of bronze.
Psalm 18v34

Are you worrying about anything that is deflecting from the fullness that

God has in mind for you and your life? What is causing you to crumble or to lose flexibility and desire for the shape Christ has appointed for you? Take your worries and shape them into prayer, bringing every thought captive before Jesus who will intervene on your behalf and correct every issue that concerns you. He can re-fashion our thoughts and our heart through prayer to comply with His will and purpose.

P AUSE AND THINK about the shape you are reflecting. Is it your own will or the will of God brought about through spiritual disciplines of prayer and obedience?

R ECORD your worries, then shape them into prayers. Bring them into alignment with the will of God. Don't just worry—pray! Develop disciplines in your routine to include prayer. How about turning up to God's gym in prayer, preparing yourself for your God-appointed shape in life and ministry?

A CKNOWLEDGE that God's plan is better than yours. Tune in to His frequency through prayer and intercession.

Y IELD afresh to God and let Him sort out your programme for spiritual fitness.

37

PICTURE PRAYERS

*I look up at your macro-skies, dark and enormous, your
handmade sky-jewelry, moon and stars mounted in their
settings. Then I look at my micro-self and wonder, why do you
bother with us? Why take a second look our way?*
Psalm 8v3&4 (MSG)

GOD HAS DISPLAYED HIS glorious splendour through His created works
for every living person to see, enjoy and admire. How can we respond to
such beauty and magnificence beyond simple jaw-dropping admiration? By
pausing and returning thanks and praise to our amazing Creator.

God uses huge brushstrokes to paint a picture that reveals His nature, His
goodness, and His generosity toward us. He also takes care that every tiny
detail is in place so that not one person is able to miss His handiwork. God
has considered every need pertaining to our fullness of life and wellbeing.
When we lift our hearts in prayer in that secret place, He reveals even more
than what is visible, opening our understanding to hidden and deeper truths—
spiritual treasures beyond explanation. Are we pausing to look, admire and
wonder at the magnificence of our Creator God?

*The unspiritual self, just as it is by nature, can't receive the gifts
of God's Spirit. There's no capacity for them. They seem like so
much silliness. Spirit can be known only by spirit—God's Spirit
and our spirits in open communion.*
1 Corinthians 2v14 (MSG)

God longs to show us what we can't see with our natural eyes, but we need to make room for what is spiritually discerned. Prayer and thanksgiving open our spirit to the treasury of the wisdom of God. I have found, whether praying alone or with a group of like-minded people, that God will often drop pictures into our spirit which aid us in our praying. 'Seeing in the spirit' helps our belief. Just as "a picture paints a thousand words," God knows how to paint relevant pictures to spur us on—analogies that resonate with our spirit and relate to our world. Sometimes He will even use humour to release joy and greater confidence.

While praying recently, I had the 'sense' or a 'picture' of the devil exclaiming, "You're exhausting me, I need to have a lie-down!" How great to know we can wear the enemy out by praying and taking authority over his activities! Long may we continue to wear him out until can he do no more that withdraw in exhaustion. Another time when I was pursuing healing in prayer for a person with cancer, I saw a picture of Jesus chasing the cancer out of this man's body. This became the recurring picture in my mind's eye, spurring my faith into a more confident expectation.

Do we conjure these scenes up, or do they come in the spirit in response to a heart posture of prayer? I believe the second. Pictures from God help us visualise our breakthrough and the answers to our petitions. One scripture that was quickened to me was Psalm 5v12: "For You, O Lord, will bless the righteous; with favour You will surround him as with a shield." The picture I received from this passage was to don the shield of favour as we would a garment—that wrapping God's 'favour-shield' around us would ensure our requests for provision were irresistible. Sure enough, this quickened image became a reality as we were granted favour from an unlikely source. To this very day, I still picture myself wearing God's favour-shield to see breakthrough in seemingly impossible situations and to see His kingdom come!

P RAY with the knowledge that God wants to give you spiritual keys and truths that release healing and wellbeing. Take time to go beyond simple admiration of creation, to worshipping the Creator.

R EALISE that God wants to give you details and paint specific pictures that relate to the breakthrough you seek. One picture from God can transform a dire situation and release both faith and hope.

A CKNOWLEDGE that God invented creativity—He's not short of ideas and knows how to capture your attention.

Y IELD to God and 'linger longer' in prayer and thanksgiving.

PART SIX
PRAYER DELIVERS

Through our God we will do valiantly, for it is He who
shall tread down our enemies.
Psalm 60v12

38

CASTING CARES

Cast your burden on the Lord and He shall sustain you. He shall never permit the righteous to be moved.
Psalm 55v22

THE WORD 'CAST' HERE means to 'throw' or 'vigorously offload' any burden we may be carrying. Another way we often use the word *'casting'* is in reference to throwing a line into the sea or river in the hope of catching a fish. To draw back one's arm and cast the line into deep waters takes calculation, precision, and strength. A good fisherman then allows the 'reel to run' until he estimates it has reached the depth and position where the fish may be.

We are invited to *cast our burdens onto Jesus* in prayer, to verbally 'throw' our concerns onto Him, letting the lines of worry and even legitimate concern sink deep into the grace of God. While worries dominate our heart and mind, they have the power to weaken our faith and prevent us from fully apprehending the provision God has already made for us. But when we take our burdens, and literally 'cast' them onto Jesus—not apathetically, but with force—we find that He is well able to bear our burden. At the same time, He can sustain and steady us in our areas of vulnerability and uncertainty. Help and relief from Jesus is just a prayer away!

Do you need the steadying hand of God on your life? I have experienced God's supernatural peace and assurance when I have 'thrown' my worries and cares onto the Lord. I remember singing a popular song about lifting Jesus higher and pushing Satan lower. It was inspired by Psalm 55. The chorus is simple but strong in exhortation, encouraging us to maintain a true perspective in the midst of difficulties. It became a mantra to keep our faith in Jesus high and our fear of the enemy low.

As Christians, how we carry our burdens is critical. If we are not bringing them to the Lord in prayer, we are simply shouldering these burdens ourselves. A person who feels weighed down has the potential to become brittle and overly reactive to people and situations because they are taking the full load upon themselves. They often become judgmental toward those who don't seem to share the obsessive pressure of the burden they feel.

It is a normal human response to react to pain and pressure in a negative or alarmed manner, but we must not linger in this state. Instead, we are exhorted to cast our concerns onto Jesus, knowing He promises to sustain us and support us! As we choose to push Satan lower and lift Jesus higher, we will experience our soul being restored by a new hope and peace.

If we refuse to release our burdens onto Jesus and insist on handling them in our own strength, we forfeit the supernatural peace and power God is so willing to impart. Sadly, many people wear burdens like a badge, a form of identity to gain attention and merit. Others use burdens to excuse inappropriate behaviour or justify a constant heavy spirit. In reality, it simply looks like what it is: a burden carried without God's grace!

The good news is that we don't have to live burdened 'beyond measure'. As we travel through the initial stage of shock, pain or distress, we can confidently off-load every burden onto Jesus. Come, throw your burdens onto Jesus today!

Therefore, since we are surrounded by such a great cloud
*of witnesses, let us **throw off** everything that hinders*
and the sin that so easily entangles and let us run with
perseverance the race marked out for us.
Hebrews 12v1 (NIV)

God calls us to overcome the odds by *casting off* every excessive and obstructive weight. Today, let's run our race with freedom and endurance!

PAUSE AND REFLECT. Is there any burden, anxiety or concern that you are finding too heavy to handle?

RECORD any lingering burden that needs to be forcibly cast onto Jesus.

ACKNOWLEDGE that God is the One who has the answers, and through His grace deal with every issue. Purposefully push Satan lower!

YIELD praise and thanksgiving to Jesus, lifting Him higher, and prepare yourself for some supernatural answers and breakthroughs!

39

SPEAK TO THE BREATH

And when He had said this, He breathed on them and said to
them, "Receive the Holy Spirit."
John 20v22

IN THE NATURAL, AIR needs to be inhaled and then expelled from the lungs
if we are to survive. It is the same in the spirit realm—we need the breath of
God within us if we are to exist in Him and fully live out the abundant life He
has promised. Jesus breathed His spirit into the disciples after finding them
faint hearted and 'in hiding' just after He had risen from the dead. With that
breath, fresh courage and conviction entered their spiritual lungs, motivating
them once more, and propelling them into their God-designed future.

Much instruction is designed to speak to the minds of people and is
very beneficial, but only the Spirit of God can speak effectively to the *breath*.
After all, the essence of life comes from our Father in heaven, who is *Spirit*!
Today, many people are languishing under pressure and finding it difficult to
outwork their purpose. It's as if their spiritual breathing becomes laboured
because of anxiety. They may be breathing, but they are not living in the
fullness and satisfaction of what God has planned for them.

Why live this way, simply surviving, when we can soar and thrive in God?
True life is in the Spirit. Like Ezekiel in the Old Testament, let's be those who
speak to the breath, waking people up to their destiny and fullness of life
in Christ!

He said to me, "Prophesy to the breath, prophesy, son
of man, and say to the breath, 'Thus says the Lord God:

"Come from the four winds, O breath, and breathe on
these slain, that they may live.""
Ezekiel 37v9

In this passage, the nation of Israel collectively yielded to a spirit of hopelessness; they had lost heart, hope, direction and courage, and were now just a valley of bones, dry and lying scattered. But through the prophesying of Ezekiel, they came together, rising as a mighty army full of vitality and readied for battle. They had been infused with courage and conviction through the breath of the prophetic word!

Is there anyone you can think of who may need a word of encouragement and command through prophetic prayer? You can tell what people are *inhaling* by what they *exhale* into their environments through their conversation, attitude, and general demeanour. Is there someone who can be enabled to stand up again with renewed hope?

Prophecy is an impartation into the core of another's being, awakening their spirit to life and revelation. Jesus has prophesied over us and declared prosperity over our lives as His anointed children. Prophecy should add depth and flow to our natural breath, taking away the labour and replacing it with ease. Are we prophesying in our praying? Are we calling things to life by speaking and declaring the Word of God to them?

I have found prophetic keys in prayer that are powerful to unlock troublesome situations and renew a healthy flow in the spirit. One area Bruce and I have consistently prayed about, is our heart regarding our financial situation, ensuring our vision is not restricted by the worldly lens of our income (or sometimes, the lack thereof). Instead, we place our faith and hope in God, who has access to any means necessary, for the sake of ministry. There have been times when God has directed us to give in response to prophecy even when we could least afford to. But eager obedience to the word of direction always broke open the heavens and released resources supernaturally.

Even while writing our previous books, we were sustained by faith as we waited to see where the finances for publishing and printing would come from.

God blessed us more than we could imagine as we watched money flow in from unexpected sources. What an amazing testimony to recall!

> *So I prophesied as I was commanded; and as I prophesied,*
> *there was a noise, and suddenly a rattling; and the bones came*
> *together, bone to bone. Indeed, as I looked, the sinews and the*
> *flesh came upon them, and the skin covered them over; but*
> *there was no breath in them.*
> *Ezekiel 37v7&8*

We can either crumble beneath the spirit of hopelessness, as Israel did, or we can prophesy to our situations. Supernatural things happen when we prayerfully prophesy!

P RAY AND PROPHESY what you sense God has released into your spirit to bring breakthrough.

R ECORD the prophetic revelations you have received, and speak them out in prayer, using your voice to impart faith, hope and courage into situations that seem lame and hopeless.

A CCEPT the anointing of God to help you rise up and speak words of authority that will break spiritual strongholds and despair.

Y IELD to God in prayer and listen more intently to what He is saying regarding certain people and situations. Then pray accordingly!

40

PRAYER OF ANOINTING

Behold, I send the Promise of My Father upon
you; but tarry in the city of Jerusalem until
you are endued with power from on high.
Luke 24v49

THE BIBLE LIKENS 'ANOINTING' to oil being rubbed into our skin, leaving it supple and soft. How soothing! Why would we not want the anointing of God?

The anointing results in us being soft in spirit, yet sharp and precise in prayer and in ministry as we operate in the spiritual gifts He has graced our lives with. As God's children, we need to ask for sharper discernment and perception if we want to see God move in power. We do this by being in prayer, allowing the Holy Spirit to fill us and fine-tune our spiritual gifts.

If the ax is dull, and one does not sharpen the edge, then he
must use more strength; but wisdom brings success.
Ecclesiastes 10v10

Anointing speaks to our need of an endowment of power from on high and acknowledges God's supremacy. It brings understanding and an ease of movement to our life. It helps us to effectively minister into the lives of others, to witness change and breakthrough even in difficult situations. This kind of anointing embraces the same quality, ability, and power that Jesus ministered with here on earth!

While on earth, whoever Jesus touched was set free. Imagine that! The power of the Holy Spirit was upon Him while He healed and set people free through supernatural exploits . . . and Jesus was successful in His mission! We read that God anointed Jesus of Nazareth with the Holy Spirit of power as He went about doing good and healing all those who were oppressed by the enemy (Acts 10v38).

Jesus operated in the anointing He had received! When we are passionate to see God's power at work in the same manner Jesus was, we will seek His presence and His anointing on our lives through prayer. So many Christians today are labouring and struggling when the anointing of God is available to them. We just need to make ourselves available!

Sometimes, we need to wait on God in prayer for the anointing to come. To 'wait' means to bind yourself to God's Word, allowing it to be intricately woven into your way of being and operating. The disciples followed this command and waited in the upper room until they received the promise of the Father. They bound themselves to the word Jesus had spoken that after His departure, they would receive power when the Holy Spirit came upon them. Jesus knew they could not outwork the will of God by their own strength, but would need the anointing to fulfil His mission.

An anointing comes upon us in response to a strong inner witness to the word and the acceptance of God's promises. If we do not wait, we will not sense the anointing 'oil' being 'rubbed in'. The disciples positioned themselves together as they waited in prayer to receive their anointing, and they were filled with the dynamic power of God that supersedes any human effort or endeavour! When it came, the crowd marvelled at the outpouring and manifestation of the Holy Spirit—something phenomenal, beyond explanation had just happened.

> *Then they were all amazed and marveled, saying to one*
> *another, "Look, are not all these who speak Galileans? And*
> *how is it that we hear, each in our own language in which we*
> *were born? . . . So they were all amazed and perplexed, saying*
> *to one another, "Whatever could this mean?"*
> *Acts 2v7-12*

The anointing draws attention to Jesus. Have we positioned ourselves to receive it? God loves to invest His anointing into hearts that are open and hungry before Him!

P AUSE AND RECOGNISE that without the anointing of God on our lives we can achieve very little because we are working through human ability, not by the power of the Holy Spirit.

R ECORD the promises you have received, allowing them to be woven into your very being. Expect to be filled with God's power and to see God move in supernatural ways as you step out in the anointing.

A CKNOWLEDGE God's goodness and grace as He pours out His Holy Spirit in great measure. Just be still and avail yourself to be filled with His power and might. Watch how the Holy Spirit works to land His revelation within you.

Y OKE yourself to God's promises and see the oil of supernatural healing and miracles flow through your life!

41

CITIZEN OF HEAVEN

*But there's far more to life for us. We're citizens of high
heaven! We're waiting the arrival of the Savior, the Master,
Jesus Christ, who will transform our earthy bodies into
glorious bodies like his own. He'll make us beautiful and
whole with the same powerful skill by which he is putting
everything as it should be, under and around him.*
Philippians 3v20&21 (MSG)

WHEN WE PRAY AS a child of God, we pray from the position of a citizen of
the kingdom of Heaven. Imagine that! Everything in God's kingdom that
is beautiful, majestic and holy, is available for us to access. We receive our
rights as a child of God through salvation and faith in Jesus Christ. Amidst
the daily skirmishes of life and the voices of opposition that sometimes rise
against us, we need to remember whose kingdom we belong to.

Paul, an apostle of Jesus, knew his rights as a Roman citizen when he
was arrested by the authorities of the day, who strongly accused him and
challenged the validity of his ministry.

*The commander ordered him to be brought into the barracks,
and said that he should be examined under scourging . . . and
as they bound him with thongs, Paul said to the centurion
who stood by, "Is it lawful for you to scourge a man who is a
Roman and uncondemned?"*
Acts 22v24&25

Historically, 'scourging' was a form of punishment—the binding and

134

whipping of a prisoner with the intent to oppress, silence, and afflict painful physical suffering. Paul, however, knew his rights as a Roman citizen. He knew that cross-examination by cruel and barbaric actions was contrary to Roman law. On hearing this, the centurion relayed Paul's claim promptly to the commander. In Acts 22v26-29 we read:

> When the centurion heard that, he went directly to the captain. "Do you realise what you've done? This man is a Roman citizen!" The captain came back and took charge. "Is what I hear right? You're a Roman citizen?" Paul said, "I certainly am." The captain was impressed. "I paid a huge sum for my citizenship. How much did it cost you?" "Nothing," said Paul. "It cost me nothing. I was free from the day of my birth." That put a stop to the interrogation. And it put the fear of God into the captain. He had put a Roman citizen in chains and come within a whisker of putting him under torture! (MSG)

The authorities knew that they would be in violation of the rights of a Roman citizen if they were to lay a hand on Paul. Likewise, the enemy of our soul knows he is in deep trouble when he seeks to assault those who are citizens of heaven. As a citizen of heaven, we need to speak up and exercise the rights we have in the name of Jesus, telling the enemy to back off when he attempts to assault, intimidate or torture us. We rightfully belong to Jesus and His kingdom!

The enemy will try to overwhelm and confuse us to make us stumble. In these moments we need to remind Satan to whom we belong and acknowledge our rights as God's children. We need to tell Satan that he cannot touch our body, our faith, or our family. When we are living in harmony with kingdom principles, we can be assured that God will defend us.

> "No weapon formed against you shall prosper, and every
> tongue which rises against you in judgment you shall
> condemn. This is the heritage of the servants of the Lord,
> and their righteousness is from Me," says the Lord.
> Isaiah 54v17

Instead of permitting the enemy to punish us, let's tell Satan who we are and where to go, reversing every curse and sending it back to where it came from!

P AUSE AND REFLECT on your position and rights as a citizen of heaven.

R ECORD all the benefits you have received as a child of God and citizen of heaven. Consider where the enemy may be trying to cheat you out of what is rightfully yours. Vocalize aloud, so the enemy hears who you belong to, and refute his rights to condemn you.

A CKNOWLEDGE the blessings of citizenship with Jesus and hold on tight to them. Give thanks for every blessing that is yours to claim.

Y IELD afresh to God, and strongly refuse to be knocked out of your position as a loved citizen of heaven.

42

CUT THE CORD

O LORD, truly I am Your servant; I am Your servant, the son of
Your maidservant; You have loosed my bonds.
Psalm 116v16

STRENGTH IS REQUIRED TO break the thick cords that hold us in bondage.
Jesus is the only one with the power to loosen these bonds. Sometimes,
the current troubles we are struggling with can be traced back into our
history, perhaps as a hereditary sin or fear. These forces seek to push us into
behaving in a way we do not choose, leaving us feeling helpless.

Has it dawned on you, that a consistent struggle with a negative behaviour
such as anger, may not be just your own issue, but a *spirit of anger* that has
come down through generations past? Every day we may fight to overcome
sin, but if we fail repeatedly and do not experience long-lasting breakthrough,
we can fall into patterns of self-condemnation. This is counterproductive. We
either need to exercise our own strong authority in the name of Jesus, or seek
out someone with godly authority to pray with us for any hereditary chain
to be broken. Cycles of sinful and harmful behaviour can only be broken
through authoritative prayer and faith.

Confess your trespasses to one another, and pray for one another,
that you may be healed. The effective, fervent prayer of a
righteous man avails much.
James 5v16

Consistent sin has detrimental consequences; it destroys confidence and
jeopardises relational closeness. It is important to recognise any contributing

thoughts and actions and repent if we are to know a greater freedom in our Christian experience. Because we all fall short of God's glory, it is necessary for Christians to exercise the gift of repentance. King David was so bowed down by unconfessed sin that it took the prophet Nathan, through a word picture, to awaken David to the full consequences of his actions. The effects of hidden sin that David felt could only be removed through repentance. He describes his condition and the relief he experienced through God's forgiveness in the following Psalm:

Blessed is he whose transgression is forgiven, whose sin is covered. Blessed is the man to whom the Lord does not impute iniquity and in whose spirit there is no deceit. When I kept silent, my bones grew old through my groaning all the day long for day and night Your hand was heavy upon me; my vitality was turned into the drought of summer.
Psalm 32v1-4

When a baby is born, the umbilical cord is cut and the original supply from within the mother's womb to nurture the baby ceases. As the baby embarks on a journey in the outside world, they are firstly reliant on the adult figures in their life, and gradually grow up to take care of themselves. In the spiritual realm, because of strong ties of iniquity, people are often still being fed through the supply line of hereditary sickness and disease, corruption, fear, or anxiety. It is time to cut the cords that tie us to a life of despondency, depression and subjection to what has always been, and to enter the new life Christ has offered us.

Let's recognise what is feeding our spirit and choose freedom through repentance not only for our own misadventures, but for our forefathers' sins. Links need to be broken and certain ways of thinking need to change in order to align ourselves with the new mind we have in Christ. David declares in Psalm 32v6:

For this cause everyone who is godly shall pray to You in a time when You may be found; Surely in a flood of great waters they shall not come near him.

This was David's newfound confidence—that through repentance, any flow from the enemy was no longer able to reach him! I experienced this in my own life when I prayerfully took authority over a hereditary spirit of rejection that had caused me to strive for acceptance through works and performance. I realised that my sense of acceptance was strongly linked to imposed requirements. As that spiritual 'umbilical cord' was cut, I experienced freedom to pursue God-adventures with much more joy and peace!

We have the authority in God to stop any negative feed from the enemy into our hearts and minds. Through prayer, we can 'change the channel'!

P RAY TO GOD and ask Him to reveal any bondage you may have because of the iniquities of the past.

R ECORD any negative thought patterns and behaviour. Through prayer, cut the cord of negative feeds and demonic supply.

A CKNOWLEDGE that only Jesus can deliver you from sin and iniquity.

Y IELD to God with thanksgiving and thank Him for your newfound confidence.

43

WHAT'S IN A NAME?

For this reason I bow my knees to the Father of our
Lord Jesus Christ, from whom the whole family in
heaven and earth is named.
Ephesians 3v14&15

Much thought and care is given when naming a child these days. New parents often consider the meaning of the name and how it relates to the child's identity. This was not so prevalent in our day. As new parents, our choice of names was based on how the name sounded. In subsequent years, however, we did find it beneficial to learn the meanings of our children's names.

One of our sons was what some people may describe as an 'adrenalin junkie,' always taking risks, living a little too close to the edge, and worrying us with several near-miss accidents. Then one day I read that his name, derived from Scottish roots, meant, "God will protect." This meaning brought comfort to our hearts and gave relief to our spirit. Any time we felt anxious or concerned for his safety we declared out loud the meaning of his name: God will protect! God watched over our son and deployed the angels needed to keep him safe. It was not coincidence that his name meant what it did!

There is power in a name. Jesus even changed His disciple Simon's name the very first time they met, so it better reflected his God-given nature:

Andrew . . . found his own brother Simon, and
said to him, "We have found the Messiah (which is
translated, the Christ). And he brought him to Jesus.

Now when Jesus looked at him, He said, "You are
Simon the son of Jonah. You shall be called Cephas"
(which is translated, A Stone).
John 1v41&42

The name Peter comes from the Greek word *Petros*, meaning, 'stone or rock'. The name Simon, on the other hand, meant 'a reed'. This name likened Simon to a plant that swayed when any force pressed against it. Perhaps he was known as an emotional and unstable man who heard truth but was easily dissuaded. Now, however, Peter was to be referred to as someone who was 'rock solid'. Over time, he fully earned the title, displaying stability, boldness, and unshakeable faith. Jesus knew what was in Peter all along and gave him a name worthy of his future.

Your parents may have given you a name that perfectly reflects who you are and provided the scope to emulate and become all your name encapsulates. When this is not the case, God will rename you in a way that reflects the vision He has for you, a name that speaks powerfully into your destiny and future. How incredible is that?!

Maybe you have been called discouraging names in your lifetime—nicknames that have stuck and demoralised you. God is able to remove every unkind name from your heart, because they are not your identity—the name God calls you is who you are! The enemy seeks to confuse our identity, labelling us with words that are derogatory and damaging. This is why Nebuchadnezzar gave Daniel and his friends Babylonian names (after foreign gods). He wanted to break their spirit, change their heart allegiance, and force submission to himself. In Babylon, these young men were known as Shadrach, Meshach and Abednego, but in Hebrew, their names were Belteshazzar (My judge is God), Hananiah (Yah is gracious), Mishael (Who is like God?) and Azariah (Yah has helped). In the fiery flames of the furnace, those Jewish boys remembered their Hebrew names and emerged unscathed and unharmed from the enemy's fire.

Throughout the Bible, God changed people's names to fit their God-given inheritance. The same is true for us. There is a God-given grace on our names, allowing us to fulfil a specific destiny. Our names are powerful! Let's prayerfully call forth the destiny of people and communities by using the name God has granted them!

P AUSE AND REFLECT. How do you view yourself? What name are you called by?

R ECORD any harmful names or nicknames that have had a significant impact on your behaviour. Then take authority over all those negative labels in the name of Jesus!

A CKNOWLEDGE who and what God has called you and imagine yourself accordingly. Speak out God's name over your life in prayer, consistently reminding yourself who you truly are.

Y IELD in faith to the identity you have in Christ. You are a beloved child of God, born for a purpose, and living to His praise!

44

TRAVAIL

*Let the priests, who minister to the Lord, weep between the porch
and the altar; Let them say, "Spare Your people, O Lord, and do not
give Your heritage to reproach, that the nations should rule over them.
Why should they say among the peoples, 'Where is their God?'"*
Joel 2v17-19

IN THE OLD TESTAMENT, the priests took responsibility for the people's
welfare, carrying the weight and burden of Israel's sin before the altar of
God. Beginning at the porch of the temple, they moved in prayer, weeping
over the nation's disobedience because it could subject Israel to captivity
by heathen nations who would mock Israel's demise. The priests implored
God for mercy to spare Israel from these threats of ungodly rule and
domination. Our hearts too should weep for the state of the nations and
the state of human hearts. Many people are distant from God's original plan
and purpose. The pain of rampant sin and blatant pride should cause us to
travail in prayer for God's mercy.

To *travail* involves engaging in a painful and laborious effort to see change.
We do this in prayer, knowing that, unlike the Old Testament priests, we can
come *directly* before God's throne (Hebrews 4v16). In scripture, Jesus warns
there is a coming day of great reckoning on the earth. He says:

*Watch therefore, and pray always that you may be counted
worthy to escape all these things that will come to pass, and to
stand before the Son of Man.*
Luke 21v36

Until Jesus returns, we have a responsibility to *travail in prayer* for conditions to change. We are to labour to see God's ways birthed into the hearts and lives of men, women, boys and girls. Scripture often encourages us to 'watch and pray'—not just to be aware of the enemy's tactics, but to be conscious of the moving of God's Spirit to counteract demonic forces and usher in His kingdom. Let's not allow the conditions around us to lull us into a sense of powerlessness. Our prayers hold weight! They are powerful weapons against evil and are anointed by the Holy Spirit. *Our prayers can turn the tide!*

Paul the apostle saw the tide turn through prayer. He had come against much opposition, particularly in Ephesus, where a riot broke out because of him and his companions. We read:

> *We felt like we'd been sent to death row, that it was all over*
> *for us. As it turned out, it was the best thing that could have*
> *happened. Instead of trusting in our own strength or wits to*
> *get out of it, we were forced to trust God totally . . . You and*
> *your prayers are part of the rescue operation—I don't want*
> *you in the dark about that either. I can see your faces even*
> *now, lifted in praise for God's deliverance of us, a rescue in*
> *which your prayers played such a crucial part.*
> *2 Corinthians 1v9-11(MSG)*

Paul acknowledged that the Corinthians contributed greatly to their safe release through their partnership in prayer. As we labour in prayer together, we can change outcomes and, like Paul, give God the glory!

P RAY CONFIDENTLY, knowing your prayers are part of God's rescue operation.

R ECORD your tearful and laborious prayers, knowing that they can bring about change and new life.

144

ACKNOWLEDGE that you have access to the throne of God where, in response to your faith, He will move with power.

YIELD to the spirit of intercession, and travail confidently in prayer!

45

HONEST AND FREE

*I'm determined to watch steps and tongue so they won't land
me in trouble. I decided to hold my tongue as long as Wicked is
in the room. "Mum's the word," I said, and kept quiet. But the
longer I kept silence the worse it got—my insides got hotter and
hotter. My thoughts boiled over; I spilled my guts.*
Psalm 39v1-3 (MSG)

IN SOME INSTANCES, SILENCE is the better choice. However, if we do not
have a safe outlet for our feelings, they can build up internally, causing an
unexpected overflow—and not always in the best manner! That is why we
must keep in constant communication with God: it helps our heart remain
free and our spirit open. We are not always aware of frustration or contempt
building within us, especially when we are trying to have godly responses.
But unchecked frustration will always find a way to boil over—usually in an
unhealthy, unhelpful manner.

Prayer keeps us aware of our inner feelings and helps us perceive niggles
of frustration that may be residing subconsciously in our hearts. Prayer is
where we unload our concerns and seek God's wisdom and forgiveness in
pressure-cooker situations. What a mess negative emotions can make! I am
sure we all have regretted an unexpected outburst at some time in our lives
when, like a shaken bottle of carbonated drink, what was inside us rapidly
bubbled up and spewed out. Perhaps there were issues that bothered us,
shocked us, or even offended us, and although we tried to keep our emotions
in check, they escaped through our words and actions.

Prayer keeps our hearts free. As we communicate honestly with our heavenly Father, who sympathises with our weaknesses and puts up with our shortcomings, He helps us cope with strained and difficult situations. Talk to Him—we can be honest with Him! God knows what we are thinking and feeling before we even speak, but for our own sake, we need to voice these concerns before Him. Without regular communication with God, we won't know where our heart is at, and if pressure is building on the inside, we will eventually explode.

Prayer keeps us honest. We cannot ignore or deny attitudes and pent-up emotions at the same time as we worship our holy God. In fact, through prayer, God in His love will spotlight any suppressed emotions so we can deal with them. Maybe we would rather not know what lies beneath the surface, but if negative feelings are left to marinate in our hearts, the enemy will wait for the right occasion to put pressure on us and cause us to stumble. The psalmist was so keen to maintain a free heart that he prayed this dangerous prayer:

> *Search me, O God, and know my heart; Try me, and*
> *know my anxieties; And see if there is any wicked way*
> *in me, and lead me in the way everlasting.*
> *Psalm 139v23&24*

David knew that hidden sin and unaddressed emotions could not only affect others in a harmful way but block God's blessings for his life. He wrote:

> *If I regard iniquity in my heart, the Lord will not*
> *hear. But certainly God has heard me; He has*
> *attended to the voice of my prayer.*
> *Psalm 66v18&19*

On one occasion God revealed to my heart an area of disappointment that was sitting undetected. At the time I had been wondering why God didn't appear to be favouring us in a certain area. Thankfully, God highlighted an attitude in me that was incompatible with the faith I carried. Through scripture He showed me that He would continue to restrain blessing on our lives in that area until I dealt with this conflict in my soul. Our heavenly Father desires to unburden us of anything too heavy for us to carry. So talk to Him today! Prayer keeps your heart free!

P AUSE AND RECOGNISE if any pressure has built up within you that has not yet been released to God. Realise how dangerous that can be to yourself and others.

R ECORD any feelings of discontent. Then record the truth God is wanting to reveal in response.

A CKNOWLEDGE that God knows all things and will spotlight hidden areas in your heart.

Y IELD to God's wisdom, knowing He will provide keys to keep your heart free.

PART SEVEN
PRAYER REDEEMS

Praise the Lord, O Jerusalem! Praise your God, O Zion! For
He has strengthened the bars of your gates; He has blessed
your children within you. He makes peace in your borders,
and fills you with the finest wheat.
Psalm 147v12-14

46
—

PRAYER DREAMS

*I will stand my watch and set myself on the rampart, and watch
to see what He will say to me, and what I will answer when I am
corrected. Then the Lord answered me and said: "Write the vision
and make it plain on tablets, that he may run who reads it."*
Habakkuk 2v1&2

Prayerful meditation opens our spirit to dreams God may decide
to send our way! I believe we dream 'God-dreams' more than we realise.
Dreams have the ability to awaken us to new realities in the spirit. They also
alert us to actions we need to take in order to experience breakthrough.

In the Bible we read about '*dreamers*,' Joseph the son of Jacob being one of
them. Joseph gained the nickname of *Dreamer*, not only because he shared the
dream he received with his brothers, but because his general disposition leaned
toward meditation and prayer. Even so, Joseph was positioned strategically
by God to deliver an entire nation from famine and extinction.

Not everyone will understand our God-dreams. Certainly Joseph's brothers
didn't! People may be dismissive of our dreams, and potentially sceptical, but
to receive a God-dream, know a God-dream, and outwork a God-dream, is
to discover His power at work and His faithfulness to bring the dream about.

We tend to describe things in life as 'dreamy' when they are easily attained
or assist us to simply float through life, transporting us to desired destinations.
This is seldom the reality, however, as dreams need contending for; they
require us to press into God in prayer.

Do you view dreams as a way out? They certainly can be! Maybe we
think we can superimpose a God-dream over some previous nightmare that

plays out in our life and mind. But this is not the case. Any bad dream not properly dealt with has the potential to show through, regardless of what we place over the top of it. Ultimately, Jesus is the only true way of escape, as scripture expounds.

A dream is an entry point into a new reality, a pathway into a better future. Sometimes the fulfilment of a dream comes quickly; at other times it may take a while. But in the meantime, God shapes us to fit the dreams He gives us. God-dreams often have a price tag; they require us to let go of limiting mindsets and common hindrances which could prevent their fulfilment.

So, what do we do? We pray into the dream! We lean into the promise! And we trust God's timing!

Our regular nightly dreams may consist of scrambled images from the day's activities, or concerns for upcoming events. Other dreams may seem totally unrelated to anything. But then there are *God-dreams*—the dreams that grab our attention, awaken our spirit, and release hope and faith for the future. God-dreams may even come in the form of a warning so we can protect ourselves from potential harm. In dreams, God may be alerting us to unseen needs, or giving us specific instruction related to a healing or deliverance He wants to outwork through us. There is 'bread' in God-dreams—substance and sustenance—despite prevailing circumstances.

Then there are *visionary* dreams. These can come about even in our wakeful moments when God extends our vision beyond the here and now—it is as if, as we walk, Jesus 'broadens the ground' under our feet.

> *You enlarged my path under me, so my feet did not slip.*
> *Psalm 18v36*

A God-dream is a revelation of the future, a pathway toward the promise, and an anchor in the storm. It is where God takes centre stage, invoking worship from the deepest place of our hearts and releasing whatever is required for the outworking of His plan and purpose.

P AUSE AND CONSIDER which of your dreams may be from God, requiring you to rise to a new level of faith.

R ECORD your dreams. They have an appointed time, but you can choose today to walk in prayer toward the fulfilment of them!

A CKNOWLEDGE that these dreams are going to take faith and effort to pursue. They are a pathway into a better future, but you will only apprehend the fullness of these dreams by discarding limited mindsets and exaggerated excuses.

Y IELD yourself to God. Walk out of any 'nightmare' you have been entertaining, and enter into communion with God.

47

FOCUS

*Have mercy upon me, O God, according to Your
lovingkindness; according to the multitude of Your tender
mercies, blot out my transgressions. Wash me thoroughly
from my iniquity, and cleanse me from my sin.*
Psalm 51v1&2

GENUINE AND SINCERE REPENTANCE brings focus to our lives. It is impossible to fully perceive God's best when sin and regret are occupying space in our heart. According to Psalm 51, we can experience amazing freedom in God because of His amazing love, kindness and mercy. Why would we want to deny ourselves the chance of a clean slate and a clear conscience? God is so willing to forgive! It is we who are often less willing to receive.

At times, the devil has worked overtime on the regrets I have felt about my failures. Though God forgives, we can tend to hold ourselves hostage to our mistakes. You don't need to look too widely to hear people giving voice to their regrets, lamenting over things said or done that were not edifying or God-glorifying. The good news is that God forgives—but we need to respond in agreement to His pardon. God releases us completely, but *we* are often the ones who remain bound by the chains of self-condemnation.

Praise has a wonderful way of releasing us from self-condemnation. I think of one worship song that speaks of the dead coming alive and chains that have bound us falling away as we praise. The exhortation in this song is to let go of the chains and to come out of the grave of hidden regrets.

In John chapter 11 we read of a man by the name of Lazarus. This man was well and truly dead; yet when Jesus called his name, he came alive and was released from the grave clothes that bound him.

Today Jesus is calling us out of our 'stuck' places. He removes the guilt and shame that have clothed us, and delivers us from any notion that we are still deserving of punishment and heavy sentencing.

Through faith, let go of regret, knowing that God has chosen to blot out all our transgressions! *Remission of sin is immediate, but renewal of our mind often takes time* as we meditate on God's truth and our righteousness. David was grateful for forgiveness, but he desired deeply to live with a cleansed conscience. In Psalm 51v2, we read his heartfelt cry: "Wash me thoroughly from my iniquity and cleanse me from my sin."

In this passage, David is crying out to be purged with hyssop. This plant was known for its cleansing effect on plagues, leprosy and chest ailments. Symbolically, it was known for the cleansing of the soul. David did not want the disease of sin to cling to him!

Is it time for you to cry out to God, break the chains of the past, and walk free? David knew that the cleansing and restoration of his soul would bring renewed hope and focus. Joy is a result of forgiveness received. In place of brokenness and pain, David acknowledged there would be healing and joy. Through his renewed desire, he knew creativity would be restored to his soul, helping him to maintain a steadfast spirit.

Are we recipients of the creative desires and inspiration of God? If not, maybe our creativity is being impaired through retained regret. David passionately expressed his desire to stay connected, to be full of the Holy Spirit—he implored God not to cast him aside. Being cast aside is never God's intention; no one is a 'throw away' in His sight. God is not done with any one of us, but waits eagerly to redeem and renew us. If we feel we have been cast away, perhaps there is a divide in our own heart that needs healing.

Let's desire the fullness of the Holy Spirit. Let's remember to focus on God's goodness rather than our wrongdoing. Let's not focus on regret but wear redemption joyfully!

P RAY AND CONFESS to God any area that you continue to struggle with. Acknowledge any chains of regret.

R ECORD what needs to change within so that God's clear vision and creativity can be fully released in your life. His forgiveness is powerful to save and deliver!

A CKNOWLEDGE that only God can truly cleanse your heart and give you a brand-new start.

Y IELD to God with thanksgiving, and set your focus on Him.

48

FINE-TUNE

Companions as we are in this work with you, we beg you,
please don't squander one bit of this marvellous life God has
given us. God reminds us, I heard your call in the nick of
time; the day you needed me, I was there to help. Well, now
is the right time to listen, the day to be helped. Don't put it
off; don't frustrate God's work by showing up late, throwing
a question mark over everything we're doing. Our work as
God's servants gets validated—or not—in the details.
2 Corinthians 6v1-3 (MSG)

TIMING IS A BIG DEAL in our daily lives, but it works best when our priorities are finely tuned. Prayer has always been high on God's priority list. He doesn't want us to show up late for the great things He has prepared for us!

Scripture uses the expression, "in the *fullness of time*" (Galatians 4v4). In the fullness of time, when things got pretty bad here on earth, God sent His son Jesus to die on our behalf, redeem us from sin and death, and provide us with a way of escape from sin and destruction. Out of timeless eternity, God entered time! What a finely tuned and perfectly executed plan.

As a child, Jesus cut into my life. I never had a moment of doubt about the existence of God but at the right time, salvation was revealed so I could respond from my heart accordingly. God continues this 'cutting in' and 'fine-tuning' throughout our lives. In the Old Testament we witness God moving in to intervene on Israel's behalf. God gets stirred up when oppression gets too heavy for His people.

Then the Lord awoke as from sleep, like a mighty man who
shouts because of wine. And He beat back His enemies; He put
them to a perpetual reproach.
Psalm 78v65&66

God simply decided enough was enough, and He intervened. We too need to decide how to move when we discern the timing is right in God to act. Timing is important—knowing when to turn up, listening attentively, and staying in step with the Holy Spirit who fine-tunes our hearts so we will represent Him better. God wants to deal with rigid Christianity that knows the law but fails to demonstrate His heart. To know God's heartbeat is to feel and flow with the rhythm of heaven.

Righteousness will go before Him, and shall
make His footsteps our pathway.
Psalm 85v13

One way we can fine-tune our hearts is through worship. Worship is our natural rhythm; we were created to worship. If we are finding it hard to worship, we need to enquire whether something else is holding our heart apart from our saviour, Jesus. Worship fine-tunes us, centres us, calms us, and changes us. It doesn't get any better than that.

We need to understand the importance of the first beat of the bar. This is the note we launch from. People often miss the first beat—morally, ethically, spiritually—and then wonder why life simply doesn't work for them. If we get the 'first beat' in God right, the rest of the steps follow more easily.

But seek first the kingdom of God and His righteousness, and all
these things shall be added to you.
Matthew 6v33

The heroes of the faith understood the *leading* of God, and matched their footsteps to His, accomplishing great exploits in His name. God is a creative choreographer, composing sequences of steps and movements for every individual life. Everyone's storyline is different. You have your steps to dance, and I have mine! It's God who does the linking, the connecting, the sequencing, and the choreography for every individual to live out their God-given purpose.

We find what really ticks within when we allow God to fine-tune our heart, our imagination, our desires. This rhythmic beat of our heart has been waiting to be detected by an awakening in the spirit. When you tune in, you will find the *prophetic you* which is more than your capabilities, your talents, or your intellect. The *prophetic you* is God's design, fashioned long before the beginning of time.

PAUSE AND PRAY for a more discerning heart and ear so you can hear the rhythm of God for your life.

RECORD what Jesus is seeking to fine-tune in your life so you can come into harmony and flow with Him. Achieve this through prayer, active listening, and subsequent movement.

ACKNOWLEDGE His choreography and that He knows what suits your life-flow best. He not only reveals what is best and effective for individuals, but also for communities of people.

YIELD yourself fully to His best plan, and give Him thanks.

49

—

PRAYER WAITS

But those who wait upon the Lord shall renew their strength;
they shall mount up with wings like eagles, they shall run and
not be weary, they shall walk and not faint.
Isaiah 40v31

MANY OF US ARE probably familiar with this wonderful promise in scripture encouraging us to 'wait upon the Lord'. But waiting is not passive. It is an attitude of prayer that *leans into the presence of God* for the strength to persevere. As we wait in prayer and dependence on God, there is a transfer of weight, the lifting of despondency and impatient feelings, and a reminder of what God has promised.

This scripture teaches us that when we wait *appropriately*—with faith and an attitude of thanksgiving before God—our strength is renewed, and we will be able to continue on the course He has for us. We will be able to run in His purposes with God-given agility and energy, enabling us to soar above natural limitations!

This doesn't sound at all like the waiting we sometimes experience—lining up in a queue, for instance, or waiting for a result to arrive. Even so, our patience is sometimes tried. As we trust God with delays, we wait with both a sense of calm *and* excited anticipation. If we don't wait on God, we will wear ourselves out relying on our own strength. The truth is, there are scenarios that are simply out of our reach to solve. Waiting releases momentum *beyond our own understanding*. God loves a heart that trusts Him for the ultimate God-glorifying outcome!

In the Old Testament, Elijah heard in his spirit the sound of the 'abundance of rain' before there was any physical evidence. Prior to this, it had not rained on the earth for two years or more. Even so, he was able to inform King Ahab to prepare for the deluge that was imminent because the *received revelation* had given him *confident expectation*. Why was Elijah so confident? Because he had waited on the Lord for the breakthrough, and God had impressed on him when the rain would fall.

> *Then Elijah said to Ahab, "Go up, eat and drink; for there*
> *is the sound of abundance of rain." So Ahab went up to eat*
> *and drink. And Elijah went up to the top of Carmel; then*
> *be bowed down on the ground, and put his face between his*
> *knees, and said to his servant, "Go up now, look toward the*
> *sea." So he went up and looked, and said, "There is nothing."*
> *And seven times he said, "Go again."*
> *1 Kings 18v41-43*

What can we learn from Elijah? Not only did he hear specifically from God and boldly share his revelation, he also continued to pray into the revelation that rain was coming. His faith was active, and he was strengthened in the prophetic promise. While he continued to bow his knees in prayer, Elijah sent his servant to look for a cloud. The continual instruction to the servant was, "Go again"! How often do we give up at the first hurdle or sign of delay? *Prayer waits on God. It goes again!*

> *Then it came to pass the seventh time, that he said, "There*
> *is a cloud, as small as a man's hand, rising out of the sea!"*
> *So he said, "Go up, say to Ahab, 'Prepare your chariot, and*
> *go down before the rain stops you.'"*
> *1 Kings 18v44*

It was time to move. If they had not moved immediately in response to the sighting, the river would have been too swollen to cross and they would have remained on the wrong side of the blessing!

*Then the hand of the Lord came upon Elijah; and he girded up
his loins and ran ahead of Ahab to the entrance of Jezreel.*
1 Kings 18v46

Elijah ran faster than Ahab's chariot! The word Elijah had waited on and
delivered faithfully to the king was now coming to pass, and Elijah received
supernatural physical strength to move *while he waited* for the answer. We
too will find the passion and energy to run and prosper in the purposes of
God, even as we wait. Bruce and I have found God to be so faithful to answer
prayer and release supernatural energy as we have waited in prayer. Let's not
be sluggish, but diligently pray *and* wait.

P AUSE AND REFLECT. Are you are waiting well, or not? Are you in
prayer regarding the promises God has given you?

R ECORD areas where you may need to 'go again' in prayer. Recall
'the sound' you have heard in your spirit and consistently pray
it into reality.

A GREE with God's promise and stay energised by faith in Him.

Y IELD every impatient thought, and bow the knee to the God who
answers prayer.

50

PRAYER BUILDS

*Wait on the Lord, and keep His way, and He
shall exalt you to inherit the land.
Psalm 37v34*

SOMETHING DYNAMIC HAPPENS IN the unseen realm when we pray. An investment from our heart is deposited into the future wellbeing of children, families, and nations. In response to our genuine heart's cry, we can be sure that when we pray *here*, God is moving *there*. Physical addresses, geographical distances and timeframes are no obstacle to God!

We build in the spirit by praying earnestly for the redemption of the world. We are asking for people to personally know Jesus, and for healing and miracles to take place. Prayer can shake strongholds, open prison doors, and set people free. Why would we not want to invest into a powerful move of God to change hearts and lives?

*Peter was therefore kept in prison, but constant prayer was
offered to God for him by the church. And when Herod
was about to bring him out, that night Peter was sleeping,
bound with two chains between two soldiers; and the
guards before the door were keeping the prison. Now behold,
an angel of the Lord stood by him, and a light shone in the
prison; and he struck Peter on the side and raised him up,
saying, "Arise quickly!" And his chains fell off his hands.
Acts 12v5-7*

God intervened for Peter when prayer ascended to Him from the Church.

Come on, let's pray! Let's change people's worlds with our prayers! Let's invest in the wellbeing of others, contending for breakthrough in adverse situations. Someone—or something—could be waiting for us to charge heaven with our prayers!

Psalm 37 speaks of God exalting those who wait on Him. The word 'exalt' means to 'raise to a higher rank or position'—in other words, being heard more easily and taken more seriously as a result of waiting on God and keeping His ways. The psalm also speaks of inheriting the earth. We can't build anything of significance or longevity without adhering to the will and ways of Jesus. Finally, this scripture is important on a personal level. It assures us that God's character is being formed within us as we pray. Our inner conviction and character are strengthened, and our hearts are enlarged to sustain the exponential growth God wants to bring internally and externally.

Something greater than we know happens internally when we position ourselves to intercede. There comes a reinforcement of inner personal faith and discernment. God's power is at work. As we pray, He builds something strong and long-lasting *within us* that over time manifests *through us* for His glory. So let's get going! Let's change the world through prayer, and at the same time, allow prayer to rearrange us.

Is our thinking too small? Are we locked into only what we can see and understand? Prayer builds in the invisible. Recently, I took communion every day for a month as I prayed for the integration of yet another level of God's peace into my life. I didn't become aware of this new level of peace instantaneously, but I know without a shadow of a doubt that God established a fresh, new capacity within. That impartation equipped me to inherit even more of His very best for me.

Others benefit from our prayers for their welfare, their wellbeing, and their prosperity in life. Let's not hold back. Let's not reduce prayer to kind thoughts alone. Let's build in the realm of the unseen. We will see God build as we invest in the heavenly realm of prayer. Testimonies of breakthroughs, changed lives and extraordinary shifts in situations give us an elevated platform from which to proclaim the truth of who God is and what He does. Breakthroughs speak for themselves as God bears witness to His works!

P RAY, "Your kingdom come, Lord!" Invest yourself in prayer, expressing your desire for breakthrough, miracles, and change— this is God's kingdom invading earth through prayer!

R ECORD what you want to see built, both in yourself and others. Realise that God is not limited by either time or distance. Your prayers are powerful right where you are!

A CKNOWLEDGE the building that is going on within you as you pray and intercede for others. Give thanks for the construction that comes from constant investment of prayer.

Y IELD to God so the platform of faith He establishes within will bear testimony to His works. Give God glory for all His wonderful works.

51

RUMMAGING IN THE SPIRIT

But the Helper, the Holy Spirit, whom the Father will send
in My name, He will teach you all things, and bring to your
remembrance all things that I said to you.
John 14v26

HAVE YOU EVER LIVED in a house that has an upstairs attic? What a great place to store loads of treasures, trinkets, and memories from yesteryear! I am sure you would have seen such a room in a movie or read about such an attic in a book. An attic can be the messiest room in the house, full of randomly stacked memorabilia and unused, obsolete objects all waiting to be rediscovered like long-lost treasure. There may be drawers and chests that have been rifled through, the contents tipped out and strewn on the floor.

I love the parallel in the spirit. God has so many treasures tucked away that He wants us to discover—hidden truths and gems that will strengthen, sustain and satisfy us in our current season. Someone once said, "God hasn't hidden things *from* us, He has hidden things *for* us." On our part, the right timing and a greater desire to discover hidden truth is important. Desire for discovery involves *rummaging in the spirit*—feeling around in the dark and investigating, not knowing precisely what we may be after, yet able to recognise it the moment we find it.

Just as our hand closes over a lost treasure, there is a sense of our spirit embracing a truth which to this point has been elusive or hidden. Finding what we were looking for *and* stumbling across fresh truths both result in pure joy. There are gems in hidden places, and we are on a quest to discover them.

This is why we 'rummage' in the Spirit, pondering, searching, and seeking in a realm beyond what we see in the natural or have any understanding of to date. Prayer is like rummaging in the attic of the Spirit, and what we discover there will remain with us for a lifetime.

A certain man in the New Testament went searching by night to find answers to the questions and ponderings of his heart. We read:

> *There was a man of the Pharisees named Nicodemus, a ruler*
> *of the Jews. This man came to Jesus by night and said to Him,*
> *"Rabbi, we know that You are a teacher come from God; for*
> *no one can do these signs that You do unless God is with him."*
> *Jesus answered and said to him, "Most assuredly, I say to you,*
> *unless one is born again, he cannot see the kingdom of God."*
> *John 3v1-3*

Jesus didn't chide Nicodemus for coming at night but welcomed his search to know more about Himself. Nicodemus was searching in a realm where he didn't have clarity. He was seeking truth to settle his inner wrestle. Jesus responded to Nicodemus' question, emphasising that only someone who had been born again of the Spirit could enter the kingdom of heaven.

> *Jesus answered, "Most assuredly, I say to you, unless one is born*
> *of water and the Spirit, he cannot enter the kingdom of God.*
> *That which is born of the flesh is flesh, and that which is born of*
> *the Spirit is spirit. Do not marvel that I said to you, 'You must*
> *be born again.' The wind blows where it wishes, and you hear*
> *the sound of it, but cannot tell where it comes from and where it*
> *goes. So is everyone who is born of the Spirit."*
> *John 3v5-8*

Spiritual answers are found in spiritual places, and revelation needs to be sought after. The Spirit of God is willing to show us what we don't know if we are prepared to step into the unknown and 'feel around in the spirit' through prayer until we uncover what we were instinctively looking for all along. Our spirit leads us in this search, acknowledging there is more to be grasped and understood about God. Waiting, pondering, praying, and exercising faith and trust are key to uncovering the good things God has in store for us.

P AUSE AND REFLECT. How much time do you spend meditating, pondering and addressing questions to God that only He has the answers for?

R ECORD the treasures you discover. What answers and motivation are you seeking from God for present needs?

A CKNOWLEDGE that you don't always know exactly what you are searching for, but that you have the utmost confidence you will know when you discover it!

Y IELD any grappling to God, and expectantly search for and be sensitive in the spirit to receiving truth and hidden mysteries.

52

—

THE WONDER

And the Word became flesh and dwelt among us, and we beheld His glory, the glory as of the only begotten of the Father, full of grace and truth.
John 1v14

GOD'S GLORY WAS MADE manifest in the flesh in the form of a man—Jesus. What a wonder indeed! The Message Bible reads like this:

The Word became flesh and blood, and moved into the neighbourhood. We saw the glory with our own eyes, the one-of-a-kind glory, like Father, like Son, generous inside and out, true from start to finish.
John 1v14 (MSG)

There's something about the glory of God that transcends all human comprehension, eclipses human experience, and leaves us in awe of how great God is. His glory is revealed through a revelation, an encounter, an experience, or even an inner knowledge, leaving us with greater desire to dwell where God's glory resides.

Creation declares God's glory loudly; His handiwork is for all to see. How can we not be attracted to the wonder, the beauty, and the glory of our Creator? The psalmist expresses his desire for the presence of God in this manner:

Lord, I have loved the habitation of Your house, and the place where Your glory dwells.
Psalm 26v8

To experience more of the glory of God in our lives, there is a need to establish practices or rhythms in our daily routine, creating time and space for this to happen. Here are some helpful suggestions from which a meaningful prayer life can develop. On a daily basis let's make room for God's glory in the following ways:

Make time for worship. Are there times when your heart is set apart to connect with God in reverence and awe, where you lift your head and bow your knee before God? Sometimes we just need to take time to linger, to lay before Him and soak in the knowledge that the God of the universe is present and interested in us personally. Worship opens the windows of our hearts to greater revelation and manifestation of God's glory in and through us.

So, how's your worship? Worship is about connecting in heart-to-heart communion with Jesus. If we do not carve out time and space to come with a quiet heart to hear Him speak, then something else will occupy our lives— probably the worries and the cares of this world!

Surrendering to God with no agenda but to worship allows our spirit the opportunity to hear Him better and to pray more effectively. God imparts visions and dreams to those who reverence Him. Greater results and service come from a heart of worship. How about making worship a regular routine? Simply be still before God, honouring and gazing at Him in wonder!

Make time for the Word. When we make Bible reading a priority in our day, our hearts will be stirred with faith as the Holy Spirit reveals truth that is not comprehended in the natural.

Faith comes by hearing, and hearing by the word of God.
Romans 10v17

When we respond in faith to God's Word, it pleases His heart. God's Word holds wisdom for every situation we face. His Word is an account of His faithfulness, and the wonder of His love toward us. I personally love the Word of God and draw on His wisdom daily. Through God's Word, fears are settled, courage is imparted, and we experience God's breakthrough power. God is the 'again' God—the same yesterday, today and forever. What He's done in the past, he will do *again* in the present! As you read your Bible, your prayers will take on greater meaning. I am fully convinced that God's Word works. I experience the wonder of this every day of my life!

Make time for works. Through prayer, God's works become our works. As we behold His glory and see His heart at work, we are transformed and our works reflect more of who He is. Today, let the wonder of God's love, grace and power lead you into a more meaningful space of prayer.

P AUSE AND PONDER. What daily rhythm could you engage in that will lift your heart and soul before God and allow you to gaze fully at His magnificence?

R ECORD God's wonders as you experience them afresh. Thank Him for His magnificent glory as He reveals it to you, and record how it impacts you.

A CKNOWLEDGE that your human perspective is limited, and express your desire to God to know greater spiritual truths.

Y IELD your heart and time. Make time and space to simply behold God's glory.